Also by Tim Rich

Caught Beneath the Landslide: Manchester City in the 1990s
The Quality of Madness: A Life of Marcelo Bielsa

ON DAYS LIKE THESE

The Lost Memoir of a Goalkeeper

Tim Rich

QUERCUS

First published in Great Britain in 2023 by

QUERCUS

Quercus Editions Ltd
Carmelite House
50 Victoria Embankment
London EC4Y 0DZ

An Hachette UK company

A CIP catalogue record for this book is available
from the British Library

HB ISBN 978 1 52942 855 1
TPB ISBN 978 1 52942 856 8
Ebook ISBN 978 1 52942 858 2

Picture credits (in order of appearance): 1, 2, 3, 4, 9 – Lawrence Lustig;
5 – Monte Fresco/*Daily Mirror*; 6, 7 – Joe Sealey; 8 – Bob Thomas/Getty Images;
10 – Nicky Hayes; 11 – David Cannon/Getty Images

10 9 8 7 6 5 4 3 2 1

Typeset by CC Book Production
Printed and bound in Great Britain by Clays Ltd, Elcograf S.p.A

Dedicated to the memory of Sally Wheatman (1966–2022)

Contents

Foreword

By Harry Redknapp

Les Sealey was one of football's great characters. He was fearless as a goalkeeper and fearless as a person.

Les was also one of life's eccentrics. In 1994, I took him to West Ham to be the reserve keeper and then the goalkeeping coach. At the training ground, when he went in goal against the first team, he would put one hand over his eye and hop on one leg whenever he faced a free kick or a penalty. He would psyche the player out and the ball would nearly always go sailing over the bar.

Goalkeepers are a breed apart. They train away from the rest of the team; they tend to stick together among their own kind. There has to be a kind of madness in goalkeepers.

Who wants to dive at people's feet? Who wants to go on to the pitch knowing that any error they make can cost a game? They are not the full shilling. Les was mad but in a lovely way. He was great to have in the dressing room. He was a team man who would forever be geeing the players up or getting stuck into them. I cannot tell you how much I loved him.

The first Sealey I got to know was Les's cousin Alan, whose two goals won West Ham the Cup-Winners' Cup in 1965. He was a few years older than me but 'Sammy', as we used to call him, was a great mate of mine at the club. His goals at Wembley had made him a hero among the fans. We had come back for pre-season and one time after training had a game of cricket for a laugh. Unfortunately, it had been press day at West Ham and the benches we had sat on for the team photos were still by the side of the pitch. As Sammy ran after a high ball, he didn't notice one of the benches and, despite us all shouting at him to watch out, ran straight into one of them. He broke his leg. It was one of the worst injuries I have ever seen on a training ground. It finished him. He would still come to the training ground for a cup of tea. We would talk about horse racing or go to see the greyhounds race at Romford, or visit the old West Ham track on Fridays.

Les was from the East End of London, which had produced so many footballers like Bobby Moore and Jimmy Greaves. For boys like us, for boys like Les, football was all there was. You played until it was dark and then under any light you could find. There was little to keep you at home. All we had was a nine-inch black-and-white television with a three-inch magnifying glass. We only watched one channel. When BBC Two came in, my dad said: 'How are you supposed to make a choice?' But, if you had a football, you were a king in those streets.

Les's great moment came with Manchester United at Wembley when Alex Ferguson dropped his regular keeper, Jim Leighton, for Les at the FA Cup final replay against Crystal Palace in 1990. Football management is all about making big decisions. As Ferguson was under so much pressure at Manchester United, this choice was very brave. It gives you some idea of why Ferguson went on to become the greatest football manager there has ever been. He was never afraid to make the big call.

After Manchester United, Les came back to work with me at West Ham. My favourite memory of him is from one night when we played Aston Villa at home in the quarter-final of the League Cup. I'd invited two mates of mine up from Bournemouth to watch the game. Frank Lampard gave us the lead, but Villa equalised later on and then won in extra time. Afterwards, my mates came into my office for a drink. We were supposed to go out and then they would stay with me but I told them I couldn't. I was gutted we had lost and I would now need to be at the training ground early the next morning.

They were wondering how they were going to get back to Bournemouth. The last train had already gone but then Les volunteered to drive them home. It would have been five in the morning by the time he returned from the south coast but that was the kind of man he was. An absolute diamond.

An Audience

It was nearly a decade since the old king abdicated but you could still feel his presence. A brain haemorrhage had slowed his movement and speech but had not dulled his presence. You knew he had entered the room even if you had your back to the door.

He was eighty now, sitting at the far end of the table, dressed in a grey suit. There was a glass of red wine in front of him and a small court around him, one of whom would go off to place his bets. Beside him was a great, glass window overlooking Aintree. It was the first day of the 2022 Grand National meeting. His horse, Clan des Obeaux, had already won. Joe's decision to back it had earned him £700.

'Do you want to meet him? Do you want to meet Alex Ferguson?'

Ged Mason was Sir Alex Ferguson's racing partner. Joe knew his son. There was a connection.

'I wouldn't mind. He signed my dad.'

'Les Sealey was your dad? He'll definitely want to meet you then.'

Joe was ushered over.

'So, you're Les's son? You know, your dad saved my career.'

'And you saved his.'

On Days Like These

He had always loved cars. He would die in one. It was parked outside, a silver Bentley Arnage.

He was inside, working on the house, trying to get it into shape so it could be rented out. He'd start by getting rid of that wallpaper. He would pop into Southend later to see about a new kitchen.

This would be a nice house for somebody. Rayleigh was a commuter town really. On the line to Liverpool Street. Steadily rising house prices. It would be a better investment than the pub. Why he had bought a pub, God only knows. It was such a cliché. He had sunk all the money he had made from Manchester United into the Double L in Woodford. What was extraordinary about that was he had always been so careful with property. His houses were never typical footballers' houses with Greek columns or stone lions at the end of the drive. They were places he could afford. Comfortably.

He knew what had happened to Peter Shilton. In 1989, Shilton had been playing for the media baron Robert Maxwell at Derby. He was one of the highest-paid players in the game and owned five houses as investment properties. Then came the housing crash and a phrase nobody had heard before: negative equity. Suddenly, Shilton was as exposed as if Maxwell had ordered his managers not to bother with centre-halves. It was a mistake Les Sealey had not made. Well, not until the pub came along.

It didn't even have a proper pub name. It wasn't a Royal Oak, a Red Lion or even a Green Man. The Double L sounded like a ranch in Texas that John Wayne might head for in *The Searchers*.

Everybody had been surprised when a cousin of his successfully persuaded him it could be a decent investment. He barely drank and would never set foot in a pub if he could help it. Elaine had tried white wine once when she was sixteen and hated it. In all the years they'd been married she would only ever order a Pepsi Max on a night out. They were hardly Den and Angie Watts.

Once, on holiday, he had ordered a brandy and Coke. Joe had been shocked. He was fifteen then, a goalkeeper like his dad. He'd never seen his father order anything alcoholic. Didn't he know what alcohol did to your body?

Les could remember being drunk only twice. Once was at Paul Ince's marriage to Claire. The other time was at another wedding, Dion Dublin's.

When they bought the Double L, there were jokes along the lines of 'At least you won't drink the profits.' Profits might have been quite nice. A rental property was altogether better value. Safer.

The Double L was near Woodford Town football club, where Jimmy Greaves' career had come to its drink-sodden close, with the greatest natural striker England would ever produce employed as a midfielder at the age of forty. The clientele was decent. They were a long way from the Glasgow dockers and gangland characters Alex Ferguson had entertained when he bought a pub after his playing days were done. But the real trouble was that Les wasn't the man people thought he was.

He'd done some publicity in the local paper when he bought it, and some punters might have come to the Double L for the Les Sealey they'd seen on television, clowning around in goal for Manchester United, running after the referee, egging on the crowd. However, once the dressing-room door had closed, he was a different person. He became ordinary. He wanted to go home, be with his family. He enjoyed reading about the men who ruled the East End, where he grew up: the Krays and the Richardsons. He liked military history. If someone wanted a discussion about whether the Hurricane or the Spitfire had really won the

Battle of Britain, he could contribute. But he could never be 'mine host'.

It was the opening weekend of the Premier League season. He wasn't involved. He'd work on the house and then listen to Manchester United play Fulham at Old Trafford.

Yesterday, West Ham had lost 2–1 at Liverpool. Since they hadn't won at Anfield since Bobby Moore's day, this wasn't a bad result. It would have been nice to have been there. Three months on from his dismissal, he couldn't quite understand why he wasn't. He'd been the goalkeeping coach. He'd been brought in by Harry Redknapp as cover for Luděk Mikloško and to do some coaching. He had played in a couple of games.

Once, at Highbury, Harry had brought him on as a striker with seven minutes left. West Ham were one down and reduced to ten men. At the training ground at Chadwell Heath, he'd sometimes play up front in the five-a-sides. 'Go on, Les,' Harry had said. 'Run around in their area and cause a bit of havoc.' He had run around, but Adams, Dixon, Winterburn and Bould were not the sort of defenders you panicked, especially when you were a goalkeeper pretending to be a centre-forward.

His last game had been at Old Trafford. May 1997. He'd come on for the final minute. Manchester United had already won the title, and they were winning this game too. Peter Schmeichel had asked to play as a striker, and Albert Morgan, United's kit man, had got hold of a red shirt with 'Schmeichel' on the back. Alex Ferguson had told his keeper that the match might be a celebration, but it was not a circus.

Les had come on to a huge ovation from the Stretford End. They still remembered the Cup final, the game that had changed everything at Manchester United. Even when he became understudy to Schmeichel, he was still popular, still signed every autograph book and piece of paper that was put in front of him.

He was a good coach, and West Ham had some good keepers – Shaka Hislop, Craig Forrest, Stephen Bywater. There was also Joe. He was hard on his son. Maybe too hard, but you had to remember that as a goalkeeper Les thought you had to be better than anyone else on the team sheet. Your mistakes are always remembered. DVDs full of them are sold as Christmas presents.

It was hard coaching your own son. The Lampards worked together at West Ham, and young Frankie really seemed to dislike his father when it got too much. They would go to the gym at the training ground in Chadwell Heath, and Frankie would stand in the middle while Frank kicked a football on to the wall behind him. On hearing the ball bounce, his son would turn and trap it. If he missed his cue, you could feel the tensions ramp up.

West Ham had finished fifteenth in May. In 2000, they had ended the season ninth, but after Rio Ferdinand had been sold to Leeds for £18 million in November, the results had started to slide. Even so, Harry's sacking had come out of nowhere. It had been the end of the season. There had been rows about money and transfer budgets. Harry had given an interview to a West Ham fanzine called *Over Land and Sea*, in which he said that the West Ham chairman, Terry Brown, 'didn't know how to add up'. Given that Brown was an accountant, that was quite an accusation. Brown was an avid reader of *Over Land and Sea*, and it stung him more than if it had been in the *Daily Mail*. Very soon it *was* in the *Daily Mail*. There was another row. Harry was sacked.

Les was fired a few days later. It was the day he picked up Joe from the airport after a holiday in Kos.

'How you doing, Dad? Everything all right?'

'I got sacked today, son.'

Stephen Bywater seemed especially upset. Harry would get himself another job and, when he did, he might take Les with him. But it wouldn't be like at West Ham, where the training ground was just a few miles from Les's home. Harry lived in Dorset. Les might have to move. Perhaps it wouldn't be so bad. He might have been fired by the club he grew up supporting, but they had paid him off – £96,000. It must not be frittered away as the Manchester United money had been frittered away.

Most of the day had been spent removing the old brown paintwork from the doors. The air hung heavy with dust. It had been a good idea to hire the sander, but it was hard work. Les's left arm ached, which was odd because he had been holding the sander with his right. So did his jaw, which tingled like he had bitten down hard on an ice cube.

It had been his cousin, Alan, who had got him the job at West Ham. Alan was fifteen years older than Les. He'd played for West Ham as a midfielder when Harry Redknapp was starting out at Upton Park. He and Les had both won the Cup Winners' Cup – Alan in 1965, and Les twenty-six years later with Manchester United. That would be something for *A Question of Sport*: 'Name the two members of the same family who have won the Cup Winners' Cup with different clubs.'

Alan had died five years ago. A heart attack at the age of fifty-three. He'd been working at Romford Greyhound Stadium. He loved the dogs and had a greyhound of his own, which Les then had to look after. Unlike his cousin, he had no interest in dogs and kept the greyhound in kennels at Romford until it could be sold. He had also sold Alan's car, which would have been easier had it not had a hole in the exhaust that made a racket as the vehicle clattered up Loughton High Street.

Actually, Les had been the answer once on *A Question of Sport*. It was a few years ago. David Coleman had asked: 'Who is the only man to have won the FA Cup having only played in the final?' That was him. Les Sealey, 1990.

It nearly wasn't him. In the replay of the 1970 Cup final between Chelsea and Leeds, Don Revie had done what Alex Ferguson would do twenty years later: he dropped his goalkeeper. Gary Sprake had made way for David Harvey. Nobody really remembered it because Leeds had lost, and in any case Revie's job had not depended on the result. Ferguson's had.

Sometimes, Les allowed himself to wonder what would have happened had Manchester United lost. His name wouldn't have appeared on *A Question of Sport*, obviously. Ferguson would have gone. Equally obviously. It was supposedly the win over Nottingham Forest in the third round that had saved him. It was a nice story, made better by the fact that Ferguson and Brian Clough disliked each other, but it wasn't true. The FA Cup had been the last thread holding Alex Ferguson in place. Once it snapped, it would have been over. Not even Bobby Charlton would have been able to keep him in office.

Les had read Ferguson's autobiography a couple of years ago, published after United had won the Treble. Then, Ferguson was untouchable, a god in Manchester and friends with Tony Blair – a friendship that would be rewarded with a knighthood and photo opportunities at the Labour Party Conference. He had written that dropping Jim Leighton for Les Sealey had been 'an animal instinct'. That was true. At the time, Ferguson was a cornered dog with one leap left.

Sometimes Les would sit down with a cup of black coffee, which he drank too much of for Elaine's liking, and mentally sketch out who would have taken over. Bobby Robson, once the World Cup was out of the way? He'd already said yes to PSV Eindhoven, and Bobby wasn't the kind of man to rip up a contract. Terry Venables and George Graham were too dug in at Tottenham and Arsenal. Howard Kendall had been the favourite to take over at the start of that season, but he'd chosen Manchester City. Impossible now.

The man who would have taken over was the man who had beaten Ferguson at Wembley. Steve Coppell. Young, good with the press, played attractive football and a former Manchester United player. It was obvious when you thought about it. And Les did think about it.

His arm still felt like a deadweight. It was hot and airless in the house. His T-shirt clung to him. It hadn't been that warm when he set out for Rayleigh, but now his hair was matted with dirt and sweat. There had been thunderstorms over London for the last few nights. His head began to ache. He opened a window. He'd checked the house, and it didn't need rewiring. That was a bonus. The electrics and damp were two things that swallowed money if you bought an investment property. Once he'd done the house up, he'd see about the book he'd written. He'd talked into a tape recorder owned by a teacher, a Manchester United supporter who'd said that his story – and particularly that of the Cup final – would make a decent read. People might be interested.

He had no idea where the tapes were now. He'd done the recordings six years ago, when he was at Blackpool. The tapes were ancient even then, having previously been used for French lessons; you could hear a boy's voice reading out irregular verbs. There had also been one that had 'Greatest Hits 1982' written on it. You could detect traces of 'Come on Eileen' when you played back the interviews.

If he went back to the book, he'd say what he really thought of Sam Allardyce. He'd been too kind to him. The training ground at Blackpool had been a shambles. When he'd asked one of the apprentices to make him a cup of tea, he'd been told it was impossible – there was no kettle. He had definitely been too kind to Owen Oyston. The man who had been the club's chairman had been jailed for rape but had continued to organise everything from prison like Noël Coward had done in *The Italian Job*. Les especially liked the start of that film, the Mafia boss driving a Ferrari Testarossa through the hairpin bends of an Alpine road while Matt Monro sings 'On Days Like These'. He tried to remember the name of the Coward character who had taken the applause when the inmates learned that Michael Caine had pulled off the bank job in Turin. Mr Bridger, that was him.

Suddenly, he was punched in the chest. When he turned to face his assailant, there was nothing but an empty kitchen. There was a churning in the centre of his body. He could hardly breathe. Something was happening to him, inside.

He was not one for doctors, not one for hospitals, but instinctively he knew he needed a doctor, needed a hospital. He should phone for an ambulance. But what if it were nothing? The siren screeching, the blue light flashing, followed by a mumbled apology for wasting people's time. A joke about indigestion.

He would drive to Southend. Go to the hospital. Go up to reception. 'Sorry to disturb you. It's probably nothing.'

God, he could hardly breathe. The dull ache in his head had become sharper and was now stabbing him incessantly above the left eye.

The Bentley. It would be faster than any ambulance. Nought to sixty in 5.2 seconds. There was no time. No time to wait. No time to waste.

Inside the car, it was like a gentlemen's club. The deep leather seats gave only slightly. The fascia was a wall of polished walnut. There were five small dials, relaying everything from the battery charge to fuel levels. In front of him were the big ones – miles per hour, revolutions per minute. The dials were white. The effect was like driving something impossibly grand from the 1930s around Brooklands. Thankfully, the car was an automatic – his left arm felt too numb to change gear.

He drove through the suburban roads, squinting through the glass. Within minutes, he was approaching the Rayleigh Weir underpass. Left on to the A127 – the Southend Arterial. Dual carriageway. Heading east. Sunday afternoon. Almost empty. Just a little bit faster. The engine was huge, insistent, its need for air fed by twin turbochargers, the fuel flooding in through injection lines. She was flying now, holding the outside lane. Her speed, her size, her sheer beauty ensured any other car in her path ducked for cover.

Southend, eight miles. Then four. Searching for the first A&E sign. He could not move his left arm at all now. His chest churned. His arteries narrowed. His heart pounded. He could not breathe. He held the Bentley steady with his right hand.

Southend's skyline came sweeping into view. The dual carriageway was now policed by speed signs and hemmed in by suburban housing from the 1930s, when Southend was where you went in order to escape the East End. Here, the air tasted of salt rather than sulphur, and you could buy big blocks of pure white Rossi's ice cream. The double-fronted concrete tower of the Inland Revenue building, a job-creation project from the days when nobody went to Southend on holiday, clogged the horizon. He desperately did not want his last view to be that of a tax office.

There were signs for the airport; others for the football ground. One turn, one more yank of the arm, was all that was left. Up the ramp. He drove straight towards the red-and-white sign that said 'Accident and Emergency'. The closer the sign, the larger the letters, the more blurred they became. The great V8 engine was still now. She had made it. Good girl.

He brushed the leather steering wheel with its winged insignia, gently opened the door and pitched forward on to the warm, black tarmac.

The Self-Preservation Society

I am kicking a football in the kingdom of the Krays. It's 1968. Over there is the most famous address in Bethnal Green, 178 Vallance Road. Or, as we call it, Fort Vallance. Ronnie and Reggie have lived there since they were five. It is the centre of their empire.

I think I will always like cars. The ones that pull up by 178 Vallance Road, full of flash oiks, are lovely. Big Fords like a Zephyr or a Galaxie brought over from the United States. Sometimes a grey Mark II Jaguar hisses by in the rain.

We don't see a lot of Ronnie and Reggie – well, not as much as we used to. They have a nightclub up west, and when you pick up the paper, you can see them photographed with Barbara Windsor or Diana Dors. We have no problems with the Krays. My dad said they keep everyone in order. Just so long as you remember who rules the roost, there are no muggings and no burglaries. Kids are safe on the streets of Bethnal Green. My mum is a bit more wary. She always tells me: 'Leslie, if you see those men in suits, be polite and smile. Oh, and Les, don't you go kicking a football anywhere near that house.'

Mum and Dad don't live together. They used to live in a tenement in Bishop's Way, not far from the Mile End Road. Dad was much older than Mum. He was a lorry driver for Pickford's, and all he ever seemed to do was work, eat and sleep. When he'd completed thirty-five years with Pickford's, they gave him a gold watch. It had lovely florid writing on the back, and sometimes he would take it from his wrist and show it to me. It would glint in the light. It was a lovely watch, but even as a young boy I'd think: 'It's not much for all the driving you've done.'

Even then, when I was spending the weekends with my dad, woken at half-seven with a big pot of tea and warm rolls he'd brought back from the baker's, I knew there had to be something better than this. I didn't know what it was or where, but even when Dad presented me with a pair of adidas 2000 football boots, I knew it wasn't here.

On weekdays, I went deeper into the East End to live with my mum and her mother in Bethnal Green. There weren't many escape routes. At Mowlem Street Primary School, we had a Venezuelan music teacher. She was the most beautiful woman you could imagine. One day, she called my mother into school and said: 'Your Leslie's got the most beautiful voice, Mrs Sealey. You should have it trained.' It begged the question of where in the middle of the East End were you going to get someone to train your voice, and where would you get the money to pay for it? My mother had enough trouble feeding me porridge.

By the time I'm eleven, I know there are three ways out of the East End. You can become a thief and steal your way out. You can box and fight your way out. Or there's football. You can play your way out. A pound will buy you a Frido, a heavyweight plastic football. We can afford a pound. A pound might be the price of your ticket out.

There are lots of takers for that ticket. There must be five hundred boys in the tenements where Dad lives. In the middle is a big green space, and we play football day and night, until we look up and see our parents leaning over the concrete balconies, a cup of tea or a cigarette in their hands; it is like playing in front of tall, vertical stands. One by one they shout our names, and one by one we leave.

My dad died of a heart attack when I was eleven. I didn't go to the funeral. Mum didn't tell me about it. I never discovered where he was buried. I knew it was in Leyton, and when I was older I would visit the cemeteries there in the hope of stumbling over it, but I never came across one that said: 'William "Harry" Sealey, 1900–1968'. I certainly never saw the gold watch again.

Afterwards, I lived in Bethnal Green permanently, in a big slab of concrete that was half a dozen storeys high. The flats were like something out of the Soviet Union. During the war, we sent them trucks and tanks on the Arctic convoys. In return, they must have sent us the plans for the flats. There was a pride in them, though. Every week the families would take it in turns to sweep the steps.

I always wondered why the doors were left unlocked. It could have been because there was nothing to steal. There would be televisions, but they would be black-market tellies. One would just turn up; there wouldn't be a Radio Rentals van about. I thought it might be because of the house opposite: if you committed a crime, someone would be sent to sort you out. I don't think it worked like that. It wasn't like the wedding scene from *The Godfather*, where they queue up to ask Marlon Brando to whack someone who has crossed the line. We didn't pay protection money; we had nothing to protect. We just knew that the Krays didn't want the police around for any reason whatsoever. I cannot remember seeing a policeman in Bethnal Green. The place policed itself. The lounge at Fort Vallance was on the top floor, and sometimes the curtains would twitch back and you would see one of the Krays, in his beautiful dark-blue suit, surveying his subjects.

The flats were full of people struggling to hold themselves

together. Many had seen the tobacco, timber and sugar warehouses along the Surrey and West India Docks burn during the Blitz, and ever since the principal reason for the East End's existence had been dying out day by day. The London Docks were closed to ships in 1969, the same year the Krays fell. There were still loads of bomb sites. The area around Vallance Road was known as 'Deserters' Corner'. It was filled with men who thought fighting Hitler might not be their finest hour. Not when the British army had left all its equipment on the beaches of Dunkirk.

I always had a conscious desire to get out of the area. You knew you had to try because, without being able to say it out loud, you were terrified of sinking any lower. One of my mates, Tony Walker, wanted to be a jockey, and although we never said it to each other, we both knew there was something better out there. We got fed and clothed and were always warm, but that was pretty much it.

In 1964, Tony got himself on television, in a series called *7 Up*. You can see me just behind him as he says: 'I want to be a jockey.' He was one of fourteen children selected by Granada Television from a whole variety of backgrounds to see if they would break through the class barriers. They would be filmed every seven years to see how their lives were progressing. The fourteen were chosen by a researcher called Michael Apted, who would direct the next series. It began with Apted arguing with Tony's mother. The film crew needed shilling bits for the meter so they could power the lighting rig and cameras. The Walkers had absolutely no money, so Apted had to go out on to the streets of Bethnal Green and haggle for as much change as he could. Good luck with that. Apted would go on to direct Hollywood movies. He would be nominated for Oscars.

By the time Apted and his cameras returned in 1971, Tony had achieved his ambition and had joined Tommy Gosling's yard at Epsom. He would leave school the following year. Gosling had ridden horses for Winston Churchill. To keep fit he had trained with Arsenal and came second to the eighteen-year-old Lester Piggott in the 1954 Derby. Tony raced against Piggott at Kempton, which he described as 'the proudest day of my life'. He was involved in a photo finish at Newbury but recognised he was not quite good enough. By twenty-one, he was studying the Knowledge and would become a London taxi driver. He was so popular in the series that one day, when he had Buzz Aldrin in the back seat, a cabbie came up wanting an autograph. The signature he wanted was not that of the second man to set foot on the moon but Tony Walker's.

Miracle Men

One of the reasons I knew you could get out of the East End was because my cousin had done it. He had only got as far as Romford, but Alan Sealey had done so by playing professional football. For West Ham United. He won them their only European trophy: the 1965 Cup Winners' Cup.

Alan was fifteen years older than me. He was my dad's brother's son. He encouraged me to believe that it is possible to get where you want to be in the game. The highlight of Saturday night was being allowed to stay up to watch *Match of the Day*. I was in awe of the figures on the black-and-white screen. I considered them miracle men.

Alan was an outside right, signed by West Ham from Leyton Orient in 1961. For a long time he was on the fringes, but it was some side to be on the fringe of: Geoff Hurst, Martin Peters, John Bond, Johnny Byrne. And Bobby.

Between 1964 and 1966, Bobby Moore captained West Ham and England in three Wembley finals and won them all: the FA Cup, the Cup Winners' Cup and the one the whole country remembers. He was the best footballer in the world. He had such glamour. After a home game at Upton Park, schoolboys would gather round him and he'd throw his keys into the air, and the one who caught them would run to unlock his Jaguar. Everyone wanted a slice of him. He met Sean Connery on the set of *You Only Live Twice*. They bought a country club in Essex together, Woolston Hall.

After a home game, particularly if they had won, the team would go to the Blind Beggar on the Whitechapel Road. It was a ten-minute walk from Fort Vallance, not that the twins ever walked. The doors would swing open, and Reggie would march up to Bobby: 'We're the boys. Ain't we the boys?' The drinks would no longer need to be paid for. The West Ham lads had such a good time at the Blind Beggar that Bobby bought the pub.

One day, Harry Redknapp was buttonholed by a gangster, who said: 'Tell your mate Bobby Moore that I will cut him from ear to ear.' Bobby was never cut, but Woolston Hall was mysteriously set on fire. Another one of Bobby's pubs, the Black Bull in Stratford, also burned down. He was unlucky in that way was Bobby.

Alan was unfortunate not to have played in the 1964 FA Cup final against Preston, which West Ham won 3–2, with a goal in the last minute. His glory came the following season. West Ham weren't expected to make Wembley for the final of the Cup Winners' Cup; people thought they would lose to Real Zaragoza in the semis. At Upton Park, West Ham won the first leg 2–1. In Spain, it was thought that would not be enough. Zaragoza had five forwards who went by the name of *Los Magníficos*, but the night of 28 April 1965 would probably count as Bobby Moore's finest in a West Ham shirt.

When I was a goalkeeper, I used to say to my defenders: 'See that round white thing? Make sure it stays well away from me.' Bobby made sure the ball stayed well away from Jim Standen in the West Ham goal. Officially, Bobby had just recovered from a serious groin injury; unofficially, he had just recovered from testicular cancer. There were waves of Spanish attacks, but only one Real Zaragoza goal. When John Sissons, who had scored for West Ham in the FA Cup final at the age of eighteen, equalised, that was that – West Ham would play 1860 Munich at Wembley. These days, 1860 Munich are nothing, bobbing around in the shadow of Bayern, but in 1965 they were probably the best team in West Germany. They were a better side than Bayern, and the following year they would win the Bundesliga.

Alan juggled the ball between his hands as he went on to the pitch at Wembley, which was rammed. About 15,000 had come over from Munich, some dressed in lederhosen. The rest of the stadium was West Ham United. Alan would still have been nervous. He was twenty-three and this was the biggest night of his life. It would also be the best.

In the dressing room, Bobby had been extremely confident. It was a very young team. Brian Dear, the striker, was twenty-one. Bobby had gone over to calm him down.

'You should walk behind me when we come out.'

'Why, Bobby?'

'Because you'll definitely get your picture taken.'

West Ham are the better team, and with twenty-two minutes to go, Alan takes a pass from Ronnie Boyce on the right side of the area. He can see a defender in a white shirt coming over to cover, but he gets in his shot just before the tackle comes in. Alan is leaning back when he strikes the ball and it rifles into the top corner of the net. He celebrates with a forward roll. It is his first goal in four months. Alan's second is a killer, the ball crossed by Bobby, laid back by Martin Peters and clipped home by Alan.

The team go up the thirty-nine steps. They can hear 'I'm Forever Blowing Bubbles' being sung by the crowd above and below them. Their eyes are blinded by the flashbulbs of all the photographers crowding round, but they are still able to see Bobby lifting the only European trophy West Ham United have ever won.

The photographers are in the dressing room now. The players should be pouring champagne, or at least drinking beer, but instead they are served tea and sandwiches. Ron Greenwood never liked too much fuss. When West Ham won the FA Cup the year before, Greenwood had taken the trophy home with him on the Tube. There is a photograph of West Ham's manager sitting with it at Tottenham Court Road station. His players are paid a £900 bonus. Brian Dear uses it to buy a house in Hornchurch.

Alan's a hero now. West Ham go on tour and play 1860 Munich again, this time at Randall's Island Stadium in New York. Alan scores. They take another flight to West Germany to play Eintracht Frankfurt. Alan scores again.

There is a week to go until the start of the season – away to West Bromwich Albion. Cricket is very popular in the West Ham dressing room. Jim Standen is an opening bowler for Worcestershire and helped them win the County Championship in 1964, Geoff Hurst played as a wicket-keeper for Essex Second XI, and when he was fifteen Bobby Moore captained The South against The North in youth-team cricket; he was caught at slip by Colin Milburn.

The team decide to have a cricket match at the training ground at Chadwell Heath. The ball is struck to the boundary. Alan chases after it and crashes into a wooden bench. He hits it so hard, he breaks his leg. It takes sixteen months before he is fit to return, but he isn't the same player. The broken leg has drained too much from his game. He drops down a division to play for Plymouth. It doesn't work out, and he comes back to east London to play non-league football for Romford and find work at the local greyhound track. He loves the dogs.

*

I was seven when Alan won the Cup Winners' Cup. Our football was tenement football. We would take our ball to another block of flats and play furious matches on red ochre gravel. We would get a dad or an older brother to referee. Your block had to win. There was pride in what we did.

I would play for anybody. There were loads of teams in Bethnal Green, but the major problem was getting a kit together. Many parents didn't have the money, so some businessmen who had made good would dip their hands into their pockets and stump up for one.

One of my first teams was the Cambridge and Bethnal Green Boys' Club, which had been founded by Jewish businessmen. At first, you had to be Jewish to play for them, but that requirement was dropped in 1936, when the East End Jews were under attack from Oswald Mosley's Blackshirts. After I made it as a professional, I went back to Cambridge Green to present some awards, but much of the community spirit had disappeared. The club still had money, but the interest had gone. It closed in 1990.

At the weekend, I would turn up with my boots at Hackney Marshes, looking for a game. When I saw any sort of match with a ball rolling about, I'd ask if I could play. Most of the time they said no. Well, they didn't say no. They used to tell me to fuck off. That's how you say no in the East End.

I began playing for a team called Interwood, based in Walthamstow. They developed a lot of talented players.

Chief among them was Terry Hurlock, who turned out to be one of the hardest men ever to play for Millwall. Terry owned a pub, the Prince of Wales, and one evening, before they played Wimbledon, he invited a few of the lads round. One of them asked him how he would deal with Vinnie Jones. 'Like this,' said Terry. He got up and kicked the door until it was hanging off its hinges.

I became a goalkeeper by chance. I never set out to be Bob Wilson or Pat Jennings, but one afternoon, the Interwood keeper couldn't make it and our manager, Terry Gibson, asked me to go in goal. I liked it. I was good at it. I stayed there. I was fourteen.

The person who had the greatest influence on my early football career was the headmaster at Leyton County High School, Mr Piggott. He was always dressed very smartly and had an air about him that instantly commanded respect. I was what they called a 'wagger' – in other words, a truant. I never used to go to school, and by the beginning of my final year I was probably a hopeless case. The Education Board sent people round to my mum to ask why I wasn't at school. I would get clumped by her and then go out and play football all day.

Mr Piggott did not try and get me to realise the error of my ways. Nor did he have me counselled by a social worker. What clever Mr Piggott did was allow me to stay off school permanently. One day, he called my mother into school and said: 'I believe your son has got a talent for football, but he hasn't got a talent for academic qualifications. He doesn't want to be at school, and by making him come I am forcing him to do something that should be done but which would take him nowhere.

'Mrs Sealey, why don't we do this, with your agreement? Because your boy has got such a talent for football, there is a possibility he will make it. Unfortunately, I don't think he will make it in any other sphere of life. He is not going to be a stockbroker. To stop all the problems, why don't I mark him down as being here, but he doesn't have to come to school?'

I will always remember standing in his office, listening to this in absolute amazement. Mum was sitting down, and Mr Piggott was sat at his large oak desk. He explained he was there to help each and every child, and the best help he could give me was to let me play football all day long. He was allowing me to go and train with a professional club full-time while I was still at school. This was ever so slightly illegal and would probably have got him into serious trouble if he had ever been found out. The headmaster did what he believed was the best thing for me at the time. He looked at me and thought: 'He might just make it.'

I haven't seen Mr Piggott since I left school officially, but I hope he won a million pounds on the Pools because he provided me with the only opportunity I would ever get to make something of my life.

I went to train with Leyton Orient. They were a good team who, in 1974, would miss out on promotion to what is now the Premier League by a point. When I was in my last year at Leyton County High School, I used to go in at the normal time and get my mark. I even had the school uniform on. I then went home and would go to training. If there wasn't any, I would do exercises or go running. The only time I would stay in school was Wednesday afternoons, because it was games.

One day after a match, a tall man came over. He was wearing a worn silvery suit and had a swarthy complexion that made him look like an overgrown Comanche. He smoked Player's cigarettes constantly. He introduced himself as Derek Wood and said: 'I'm a scout.' My first thought was he was the kind of scout who would tell General Custer that it was perfectly safe to go down to the Little Bighorn. I stared at him blankly.

'I'm a football scout. I'm the London scout for Coventry City. I thought you played ever so well today.'

'Sorry. I didn't know you were a scout. I thought scouts dressed differently.'

'Oh, this,' he said, rubbing the thin lapel between his thumb and forefinger. 'This is my scouting suit.'

He had a scouting car, a gold 1600E Ford Cortina. The driver's seat was broken and held in position by a large piece of wood. He asked if I would like to drive up to Coventry for a trial. Derek said I would get a decent opportunity to prove myself. I expected that to be bollocks, but it turned out to be true.

So, one Sunday, we set off in Derek's scouting car. We travelled up the M1, exhaust fumes going out of one end and cigarette smoke drifting back from a half-open window, and with a plank of wood between us. As we drove, it occurred to me that if Coventry were paying Derek according to his results, his career can't have been especially successful, if the state of his car was anything to go by.

When we arrived at the training ground, I was immediately ushered into a dressing room, while Derek went over to Bob Dennison, who was Coventry's chief scout. I could hear Derek say: 'We've got a good one here.'

God must have looked down on me that day. I wasn't overawed by the fact I was having a trial for a Division One club. I wasn't bothered if they gave me a contract or not. I didn't have my parents on the touchline screaming encouragement at me. Perhaps because of all that, I played a blinder. The ball hit me on the hands, feet, face and arse. It did not, however, hit the back of the net. When the final whistle went, I looked over at Derek, who had a big smile all across his big Comanche face.

When we'd first arrived, I'd been pretty much ignored, but now people were coming over, offering me tea and biscuits, asking if I had enjoyed myself and wondering what I thought of the training ground. I was shown inside and steered towards a table and chair and asked to sign a piece of paper.

The Fix

I am at Euston station. It's a Tuesday evening in 1973, and I formally left Leyton County High School this afternoon. I'm sixteen, looking for the train to Coventry. A return ticket costs £4.46. That's more than half the weekly wage I will earn as an apprentice goalkeeper at Coventry City.

Before I got my bags together and set off for Euston, Mum explained that she had a few bob stashed away. She had found out how much it would cost to get to Coventry and said she would give me the price of the ticket so I could come home after the A-team match on a Saturday morning and stay until Monday.

For the first six months, she gave me £4.46 a week. I knew then, and certainly know now, that she could not afford to give me that money. Going back to London meant I could see Elaine, whom I'd known since we were thirteen. She was Terry Gibson's niece. Like most kids, we would go for a coffee together or meet up at the football. I hadn't taken her anywhere else because I couldn't afford it.

I would save my eight pounds a week from Coventry so that we could go out on a Saturday night. One Saturday, I decided to take her to see *The Poseidon Adventure*. I was dressed in my wide-lapelled pinstripe suit and a round-collar shirt – feeling like a million dollars, I might add. When I arrived at Elaine's house, she went into the kitchen to make a cup of tea with her mum, while I sat on the settee as her dad, John, watched television. He had a reputation as an East End hard man. I had spoken to him a few times but had never really had a proper conversation. He hadn't even acknowledged I was there and was just messing with the channels. I thought I had better break the ice.

'Hello, John. You all right?'

He turned to me and said: 'I don't fucking like you. I want her home by half past ten. If you don't get her home by half past ten, I'm going to break your fucking legs.' He didn't look at me again, he just turned to watch the telly.

The Poseidon Adventure starred Gene Hackman leading passengers to safety from a capsized ocean liner. The slogan on the poster said it was 'Hell, Upside Down'. That was nothing compared to the hell of continually looking at my watch, wondering what time the film would finish.

We were watching Hackman hanging from a wheel in the depths of the ship's engine room and asking God how many more lives He wants to take. We didn't know if he was going to live or die. We never found out because when I glanced at my watch, it showed ten past ten. I nudged Elaine, and when I saw the look on her face I said: 'I don't care, we're going.' God had ensured there was a taxi waiting outside.

Each time I came to pick up Elaine, my conversation with her father consisted of him saying the same three words: 'Half past ten.' He never said anything else. After three months of this, I arrived to tell John that Elaine and I would be going to the local Chinese for a meal. As he turned to me, I said: 'I know – half past ten.'

'Nah, you can bring her back when you want.'

That was my formal acceptance into her family. We married in 1980.

Back in the Midlands, I was in digs with Garry Thompson, a young striker who would have a very successful career with Coventry, West Bromwich Albion and Aston Villa. There was also Val Thomas, who didn't make it at Highfield Road but did go on to play for Hereford. His younger brother, Danny, did turn out for Coventry and won the UEFA Cup with Tottenham in 1984. I once got in a fight with Danny and started commentating on it as if it were a boxing match: 'Good upper-cut from Sealey. Thomas is on the ropes, but he's counter-punching well.' It diffused the tension.

I got on really well with the landlady, and after I'd left

and moved in with my friend Alec, his wife Chris and their daughters Debbie and Sue, I'd go back regularly for a chat. I'd usually remember to bring her a gift – flowers or a box of Milk Tray. She had really looked after me.

When I arrived at Coventry City, they had been in the top division for seven years. Jimmy Hill had managed them as they progressed from the Third Division to the First. He had changed their kit to sky blue and set up the club's own radio station, before leaving to work for London Weekend Television. In my first summer at Highfield Road, Hill was back as managing director. The manager was Gordon Milne, who had won two league titles at Liverpool under Bill Shankly. He was a young manager, only thirty-seven, who had just spent £240,000 on bringing Larry Lloyd to Highfield Road from Anfield. It was a great move, and it would be paid for by selling Mick McGuire and Jimmy Holmes to Tottenham. However, after three games of the season, the Spurs manager Bill Nicholson resigns, the deal falls through, and Coventry City have an overdraft that, funnily enough, matches exactly the money they have just paid Liverpool for Larry Lloyd. There is worse to come. Coventry's chairman, Derrick Robbins, who had been underwriting all the cheques, has gone off to live in South Africa. And attendances have been falling: they were around 34,000 in Coventry's first season in Division One; now, they're below 20,000.

I don't suppose Les Sealey was terribly high on his list

of priorities, but not long after I joined, I demanded to see Gordon Milne.

You do a lot of things when you're an apprentice. You clean the baths, you sweep the terraces, you polish boots. Other people's boots. To me, it felt like a form of slavery for eight pounds a week and the prospect of a conversation that would end with the words: 'Sorry, son, I'm afraid we're going to have to let you go.' You don't actually play a lot of football, and I'd come to Coventry to play football. I wanted to be a pro for only one year, just to see what it was like. After that, they could let me go. I'd work as a mechanic.

Milne's office was small. There was a window at about head height, giving a view on to the stands. There were a couple of telephones on the desk, which was not nearly as impressive as Mr Piggott's big oak desk at Leyton High. I said: 'I am here to play football, not to clean boots, and if you don't sign me on professional terms on my seventeenth birthday, I am going home.' Then I turned and walked out. I had been at the club for six weeks. I wasn't given a contract on my birthday, and I went back to Bethnal Green.

Coventry rang me at my mother's and told me that if I didn't come back, I wouldn't play professional football again because they held my registration. I told them I would go back only when there was an offer of professional terms.

One day, there was a knock on the door. It was Bob Dennison, the chief scout. Mum let him in, and we went to the kitchen for a cup of tea. I listened to what he had to say. I remember his accent. He had grown up on the Northumberland coast and had played for Newcastle before the war. The other thing I remember about him was that, like Derek Wood, he drove a Ford Cortina. But this was an immaculate Mark 3 GXL. Blue. I was most impressed by that. However, I repeated I would only go back for a professional contract.

You might feel I was being dogmatic and insufferable. I was still just a teenager, but I wanted to play football and, as an apprentice, you're a slave. I could have gone on doing those menial jobs, but there would have been no guarantee that at the end I'd be given a full-time contract. By going home, I was finding out whether Coventry had any serious intentions about my future. In the end, I was given a one-year professional contract. I had been out of the game for six months.

Dennison was a persuasive man. When he first approached me to sign for Coventry, I had been offered £6,000 to sign for Leicester City. They did it without asking me to come for a trial. Cash. Coventry offered me nothing. It was the same with Mick Ferguson, who was Coventry's main striker. He was from Tyneside, and in 1969, when he was fifteen, he had been offered a deal by his home-town club, Newcastle United. Manchester City, who were the FA Cup holders, were also interested. One day, Malcolm Allison and Joe Mercer, who managed City between them, drove up to speak to Mick's mum. This was doubly impressive since nobody on Mick's street in Newcastle owned a car, and Allison was driving a Rolls-Royce. Mick ended up signing for Coventry. Like me, he thought he had more chance of first-team football there.

If I am to play in Coventry City's first team, I have to get past two goalkeepers. One is Bryan King. He was signed from Millwall in 1975. First choice. Behind him is Jim Blyth. Jim is two years older than me, signed from Preston. I am third in line.

In October 1975, the pecking order changes. At Highbury, Coventry are thrashed 5–0 by Arsenal. Bryan King is deemed to be at fault for at least two of the goals. His confidence is shattered, and Jim goes in goal. In January, Bryan is recalled for an FA Cup tie at Newcastle. The result is the same: Coventry are beaten 5–0 at St James' Park. Bryan will never play for the club again. Jim is now the man to catch.

Then, in April 1977, Jim suffers a knee injury against West Ham, in a collision with his own full-back, Mick Coop. I know that if this had happened at any other time, Coventry would have applied to register an emergency keeper. But this was Easter Saturday, and the next game is on Monday. There is no time. It has to be me, aged nineteen.

Coventry are one point above the relegation zone. We are playing Queens Park Rangers, who finished second behind Liverpool in 1976 but are now in the mix with Coventry. They are ahead of us only on goal difference. The thing is, I think I've got just six weeks left at Coventry and am going to be released at the end of the season. Nobody has said anything, but it's what's not said that matters. I haven't been asked what I'm doing in the summer, because what I'm going to be doing will soon be no business of Coventry City.

I know that the coach, Ron Wylie, who played in midfield for Aston Villa, either has no faith in me or doesn't like me, because all he ever does is have a go. He is always telling me that I could do better or that I'm wasting my career. He is, however, quite perceptive. One day much later, when I was in the middle of my career at Coventry, he called me at home. Elaine picked up the phone, and a Glaswegian voice said: 'Before you put him on, can I ask you a question?'

'Go ahead.'

'How can you stay married to that man?'

'Oh, he's very different when he's home. He's not the man you see. He doesn't do all the mad stuff he does on a football pitch. He doesn't shout at people all the time. He's really very quiet. He reads books. He likes documentaries.'

'You know, now I come to think about it, that doesn't surprise me. When he gets out of the shower after a match, I can almost feel his personality change. He becomes more . . .'

'Normal?'

'Aye, that's it. Normal.'

We are all actors, us goalkeepers. We all pretend to be people we are not. To the crowd behind us, the defenders in front of us and the forwards bearing down on us, we must appear invincible. They must think it will take some shot to beat us. If they don't, we're dead. The dressing room is where we put on and take off our make-up. I am preparing for a West End debut.

As we travel down to London for the game, I know what the rest of the team are thinking. Most of them are at the front of the coach, and from time to time they glance back at me, wondering what this fresh-faced kid is doing playing Division One football. They know Coventry have no faith in me. They are probably also thinking about how they are going to protect me and stop me from having to make a save or even handle the ball.

There are only about 14,000 at the game, but to me Loftus Road seems like Wembley. It is by far the biggest crowd I have ever played in front of. It is the only crowd I have played in front of. I am amazed by how much noise 14,000 people can make.

I am a boy of nineteen. In front of me and against me are these worldly-wise footballers who are very good at what they do. At the beginning of the match, QPR are awarded a corner. David Webb stands right in front of me. He says: 'When this corner comes over, I am going to smash you right in the face.' The old pro trying to frighten the young pup. I know I have to win this battle and shout at him: 'Well, fucking come on then.' To say I am bluffing is an understatement. I am frightened to death. The corner comes over and swings right under the crossbar, just above Webb's head. I jump up and, as he backs into me, I make a relatively comfortable catch. If you've ever seen David Webb at close quarters, you might notice that he's not got the smallest ears in the world. Having got the ball, I yell at him: 'Fuck off back there, big ears.' He is a bit taken aback, to say the least.

We draw 1–1 at Loftus Road. QPR's goal is a penalty. The last time Coventry were here, they had lost 4–1. I have acquitted myself well. There have been no crass errors and three or four really good saves.

The first thing Gordon Milne says to the press is that he knew I wouldn't let Coventry down. Of course, he had another set of quotes prepared for if I had played badly. He would have said: 'We knew he was a bit young and that the occasion might get to him.' It doesn't matter what he thinks. The fact is, I am in.

The next game is at home to Aston Villa. A Midlands derby. We lose 3–2 at Highfield Road, but I play well and am named man of the match. Coventry have some big personalities, men like Terry Yorath, who will go on to manage Wales, and Tommy Hutchison, who will play in the 1981 FA Cup final for Manchester City against Tottenham and score for both sides. In central defence is Jim Holton. 'Six foot, two eyes of blue, Big Jim Holton's after you,' they used to sing at Old Trafford when he played for Manchester United. He's just arrived from Sunderland. His wife hated it there. She couldn't understand a word people said, and the beaches were always covered in fog. Jim's previous club had been in Miami. In 1993, he will die of a heart attack at the wheel of his car, aged just forty-two.

Coventry have ten more games to survive. I play in all of them, including the most obviously fixed game in modern English football. Well, the most obviously fixed ten minutes.

By the evening of 19 May 1977, football is preparing to give way to a summer of cricket, including England v. Australia for The Ashes. There are just four clubs in the whole of the Football League still playing – Everton, Sunderland, Bristol City and Coventry. One of the last three teams, who all have thirty-four points, will be relegated from Division One.

Sunderland are at Everton. We are at home to Bristol City, managed by Alan Dicks, who used to be Jimmy Hill's assistant at Coventry. Sunderland and Bristol are out of the relegation zone on goal difference. Tottenham and Stoke have already been relegated. We are third bottom. We probably have to win. The only other way Coventry can stay up is if we draw with Bristol and Sunderland lose at Goodison Park.

We are in the dressing room at Highfield Road. It's not big. Bright walls, low, dark benches and coat hangers above them, and in the middle a physio's treatment table. Someone comes in through the frosted glass door and tells us that kick-off has been delayed.

Outside, it is chaos. Eighteen thousand fans have travelled over from Bristol, and nobody can find anywhere to park. Thirty-seven thousand people are trying to get in, nearly double the usual attendance. There are even more at Goodison Park, but at Everton they kick off on time at 7.30pm. Coventry's game is fifteen minutes behind.

At twenty to nine, Coventry are safe, two goals up, both scored by Tommy Hutchison. At Goodison, Bob Latchford has put Everton ahead against Sunderland. Then, from nowhere, Bristol City come back. Gerry Gow scores, so does Donnie Gillies, and suddenly Coventry are being pushed further and further back and the night air is full of songs about cider.

Jimmy Hill is in the directors' box when he hears that, on Merseyside, Sunderland have just lost 2–0. He runs to the guy at Sky Blue Radio, telling him to broadcast the result. Then he goes to the announcers' box and shouts: 'Get it on the board.' The result is given out over the loudspeakers and on the electronic scoreboard.

Terry Yorath and Norman Hunter shared a dressing room at Leeds. Now, at Highfield Road, they are on opposite sides. Yorath goes over to Hunter and says: 'Your boys can back off now.'

The last fifteen minutes are interesting, to say the least. Coventry retire to their own half, Bristol do likewise, and a game of keep-ball ensues. The home team have a go, passing the ball between themselves for a few minutes and then hoofing it upfield for the other team to have a go. This arrangement is working fine, until Jimmy Mann, a really tricky winger for Bristol City, makes straight for our goal. We think he's joking and will pull up and give the ball to us in a few seconds. Somebody goes over to stop him, but he beats his man and is through on goal. His shot hits the top of the crossbar. Yorath goes over to Mann and asks him what does he think he is doing? Actually, he doesn't ask. He yells. Mann looks at him and says: 'Oh, sorry, I forgot.'

We go back to our game of keep-ball, the game stays at 2–2, and on the final whistle both teams embrace each other and share the beers in the dressing room.

The next day, there is a furore. Alan Hardaker, the secretary of the Football League, is no friend of Jimmy Hill. They have fought over the abolition of the maximum wage and the televising of football. Hill was in favour of both. Hardaker questions the validity of the result, but it is eventually allowed to stand. We have survived. Officially.

Shadowlands

The shower was on full. The water was pumping down, pelting the young man's body as he lay crouched on the floor. The cubicle was filled with a mixture of water, steam and tears.

The shower was the only place Joe could cry. If he cried in front of his mum, she cried and everyone in the room cried. He'd kept it together for a few days, although in the evenings, whenever he saw a car's red tail light anywhere near the house, Joe would pull back the curtain a few inches just in case it was his dad reversing into the drive as he always did.

He didn't choose the bathroom as the place to break down. He just happened to be there one morning when the tears slid out of him. After that, it would become automatic, expected. He would turn on the shower and start to shake.

He would go into the bathroom, lock the door and wait to dissolve.

It wasn't the Sunday – the day of the death, the day he picked up the phone to hear a voice saying: 'This is Southend Hospital, is your mother at home?' – that seized him by the throat, that would not let him go. It was the day before, the Saturday. The house was always busy, full of voices, but this particular Saturday afternoon it had fallen silent. Mum and George, his younger brother, were out. Joe was upstairs on his computer. Les was in the living room, fiddling with the remote.

Goalkeepers are supposed to be loners, men apart from the rest of the dressing room. Their fears are different, their margins for error narrower. They have less time for the banter and piss-taking. A football team is a goalkeeper and ten others. At Manchester United, Les had been like that, partly because he rarely drank. At a party, he could make a brandy last all night. He liked Coke mixed with milk and endless cups of black coffee.

Steve and Janet Bruce would come round sometimes, and he liked talking to his teammates, especially Paul Parker, but he also liked them to go. However, when he was with his family, Les didn't like being alone. He always wanted company. Now, he shouted up the stairs: 'Come and watch some telly with me.' Joe realised he should go down, but, really, what was there to watch? The Rugby League on *Grandstand*? There might be an old film on the other side, *Shane* or *Zulu*. Nah. He'd come down for *Final Score*.

But in the end he didn't come down at all, and as Joe lay in the shower with the water splashing off his shoulders, he realised he had tossed away the last opportunity he would ever have for a conversation with his father. They might have talked about goalkeeping. They might have talked about West Ham. They might have talked about cars. It was unlikely they would have had a deep discussion about what life meant, what it was like to be alive, but they would have talked about something.

The next day, he had taken the phone call. The house was full. It was always full. Les had invited two boys from the West Ham academy to stay with them. One was Ronnie Fletcher, George's best friend, whose parents were on holiday. Ronnie was a defender who would not make it at Upton Park, partly because he was competing against Anton Ferdinand. He would sign for Sutton United. The other was Glen Johnson. He was about to turn seventeen and was a year away from making his first-team debut. He had grown up in Dartford, which was famous for its tunnel under the Thames and for producing Mick Jagger and Keith Richards.

Jagger remembered Dartford romantically: the gorse and heather of Dartford Heath; the mist-bound marshes that seemed to him like the ones which terrified Pip in *Great Expectations*. Richards was more prosaic. Dartford was home to the Vickers-Armstrong aircraft factory, which during the Blitz made the town a bullseye for the Luftwaffe. When his family moved into a council house after the war, he said the surrounding area 'looked like a moonscape', patrolled by armies of rats.

Glen's upbringing was closer to Keith Richards' than Mick Jagger's. It was unforgiving but it was all he knew. His mother, Wendy, had brought him up alone on a council estate. That and the burden of having to cross the Thames four times a week while Wendy had to work at two part-time jobs caused Les to think that Glen might be better off with him in Loughton.

Joe passed the phone to Elaine with a shrug. It was his mother who heard the instructions to come to Southend, followed by the ominous rider 'and could you please make sure you bring someone with you'.

Elaine, Joe and George clambered into their silver Volkswagen Beetle. Soon it was on the Southend Arterial, travelling down the same dual carriageway as the Bentley had a few hours before. They did not talk, and they were a family that always talked. They thought, they wondered. Les had been in an accident. He was in intensive care. The words 'and could you please make sure you bring someone with you' kept preying on Elaine's thoughts. It could only be serious. It might be very bad indeed.

Joe wondered why his dad could not speak or get to a phone. He would be all right. He would be paralysed. He would be dead. Perhaps it would be none of those things. When they saw him, he would look up from his hospital bed and grin: 'What kept you?'

When they found the hospital, the Bentley was almost blocking the entrance to A&E. When Joe said: 'We're here about Les Sealey,' a woman ran out from behind reception and ushered them into a small side room. There was a painting of a vase of flowers on the wall, the sort of picture designed to fill a space without offending anyone.

A doctor came in and pointed to a chair that looked vaguely, cheaply Scandinavian, pine with a patterned covering, and asked Elaine if she'd like to sit down. 'I'm very, very sorry, Mrs Sealey, but your husband has suffered a heart attack, a very serious heart attack, and, unfortunately . . .'

Joe looked at the flowers, stared at them intently, catching only every third word. 'We tried . . . resuscitate him . . . do nothing for him.'

Les's heart had been beating so hard that getting out of the seat and opening the door of the Bentley had triggered the seizure that killed him. The muscles at the top of his heart had gone into spasm. Medics had run over and given CPR massages and shots of adrenaline, but they were already working on a dead man. Later, the family would be told that even had Les survived, the heart attack had been so severe that he would probably have been confined to a wheelchair for the rest of his life. Any brisk movement would have risked another attack. It would be a consolation of sorts.

The doctor asked if they wanted to see Les. Joe and Elaine nodded their heads, though George stayed away. Elaine held her husband and began shaking him, shouting: 'Wake up, Les, wake up. For God's sake, wake up.' Joe noted the bruises on his neck where they had injected the adrenaline.

They were hugging, crying, consoling each other when a nurse came back into the room and asked if someone could move the car. Joe went outside and approached the Bentley. He drove a Ford Fiesta. He couldn't find the lever that adjusted the driver's seat. Then he realised it was operated by buttons. He pressed one, and the seat tilted back. It wasn't what he wanted, but it would do. He wondered how the car started. It was only after a minute inspection of the dashboard and the area below the steering wheel that he realised the car had a keyless ignition. The V8 growled and grunted, and he eased the Bentley back into a parking bay. Then he breathed out, long and hard.

They could not expose Glen Johnson and Ronnie Fletcher to what had just broken above their heads. Elaine phoned the West Ham academy to ask if someone could come and collect them.

Glen would be taken to a big house not far from Chadwell Heath run by a couple, Bob and Val, who looked after West Ham's trainees. Glen broke down in the car. Les and Elaine had been almost surrogate parents. When he returned to the West Ham training ground, Glen broke down again. He was left alone. He spent the next few days in bed, wondering if football was worth it. He was persuaded to come back, not least by the realisation that Les, who told him continually he was good enough to play for England, would have torn him apart had he heard those thoughts spoken aloud.

Football was worth it. In 2005, aged 20, he would win the Premier League with Chelsea. Glen Johnson was not remotely religious but in the dressing room, before the start of every game, he would pull his top over his head and say a prayer for Les Sealey, the mentor who would never see him make his England debut or play in a World Cup.

Elaine suggested Joe make another call. He picked up his father's phone and chose David Manasseh, who along with Jonathan Barnett ran the Stellar football agency, which Les had helped them found. 'It's Joe. Dad's died,' were his first words. Even minutes after the conversation, they were the only ones he could remember.

Until his shoulder had been wrecked beyond repair, Joe had been a goalkeeper in West Ham's youth and reserve teams, coached by his father. For most of that time, Shaka Hislop, who had learned his football in Trinidad and the United States, had been number one. George was a first-year apprentice keeper. On Sundays, they would go to the deserted training ground and train alone. After staring at the small, silver Nokia for what seemed like an age, Joe decided to give Shaka a call. The second the connection was made, Hislop cut it, almost as if he had dropped the handset. Joe had been using his father's phone. Manasseh had already been in touch with Hislop, and when Joe had phoned, the name 'Les Sealey' had come up on Hislop's screen. Hislop imagined he had been called by a ghost.

After Jonathan Barnett called with the news, Lawrence Lustig would also stare at his phone in disbelief. A photographer with the *Daily Star*, he had been Les's best friend. Lawrence had gone to school with Elaine and liked to remind Les that 'I went on holiday with your wife before you did.' It had been a school trip to Austria. He would call Les almost daily.

Lawrence had been at Stamford Bridge, covering Chelsea's game with Newcastle. He became so distraught that he had to be driven home. For months and even years afterwards, he would see something he thought might tickle Les's fancy and take his phone out of his pocket to give him a call. And then he would stop.

Joe did not want to leave the hospital. He did not want to abandon his father. As they drove home, he sat with his head against the window as the bland Essex countryside slipped by. Les had long ceased to be an East Ender. The family now lived in the Shadowlands, where Essex blurs into London, where the East End moved to when the going got good.

In August 2001, Alan Sugar was living in Chigwell in the Shadowlands, having just sold Tottenham Hotspur, the club that had wasted ten years of his life. He could not believe how much money had been 'pissed away like prune juice', how football never respected the laws of economics he had learned among the stalls of Clapton Market.

George Walker, the one-time gangster's boy from Stepney turned boxer turned businessman who had built the Brent Cross shopping centre, was not far away in a converted vicarage. There was hardly anything left of his empire now. Black Wednesday had seen to that. He had made some money picking through the wreckage of the Soviet Union, but as he paced his garden and did a tour of the swimming pool and tennis courts, he accepted it couldn't be sustained. There was a new man in Moscow, Vladimir Putin, who was making everything much more difficult.

On the day Les Sealey died, the most famous son of the Shadowlands was at Old Trafford. David Beckham would send a free kick skimming over the Fulham wall to strike the net inches under Edwin van der Sar's bar. It was Manchester United's opening goal in a 3–2 win.

Beckham had grown up in Chingford. His father would take him to Chase Lane Park. Ted Beckham would be harder, more demanding than most fathers of eight-year-olds taking their sons for a kickabout. The boy wondered why his father didn't just go in goal and let him take shots.

When the boy grew older, they would go up the North Circular to Wadham Lodge to train on pitches of orange gravel and cinder, complete with proper goalposts and nets.

After training, he would stay behind to practise his free kicks. Ted would give his boy 50p every time he hit the crossbar with one. David's accuracy with a dead ball would soon earn him very much more than that.

In May 1990, Ted had taken David to Wembley to watch Manchester United draw with Crystal Palace in the FA Cup final. David had hung up a United flag and a poster of Bryan Robson in his bedroom window so passers-by would know that even here, in this corner of suburban Essex, there was a far-flung outpost of Old Trafford.

The replay was on a Thursday, and Thursday was a school night. Ted and David watched the game on television, and when Lee Martin's shot decided the game, the fifteen-year-old leaped off the sofa and began dancing around the front room.

David was not, however, the happiest boy in Chingford on 17 May 1990. That night, a Ford Sierra pulled up outside a three-bedroomed semi in Hurst Avenue. Even then, before the wealth of the Premier League, it was not obviously a footballer's house, although other footballers were nearby. Tony Marchi, who had played for Tottenham in their victory over Atlético Madrid in the 1963 Cup Winners' Cup final, once lived opposite. Curiously, both Marchi and Les Sealey would win the trophy in the same stadium: the De Kuip in Rotterdam. London, however, was changing. From the top of Hurst Avenue, you could see the cranes and the steel that were turning West India Docks into Canary Wharf.

The passenger got out and walked up the drive. It was an entirely suburban scene, except the man at the front door had just won the FA Cup with Manchester United. Inside was his wife Elaine and their sons George and Joe, aged five and seven. The boys' grandparents were there too, and the next morning, photographers would be at the front door.

On the Monday, Les took Joe and George to Chase Lane Primary. The parents and kids mobbed them. Pages were torn out of exercise books and pushed in front of Les to sign. Joe heard his father's deep laughter mingling with the squeals of the kids and the questions that kept being asked. There was only one question, really: 'What was it like?' All the others were variations on a theme. For the first time, Joe looked at his father and thought of him as someone different, someone famous. A celebrity. He might even go on *A Question of Sport*.

Funeral Rites

The suddenness of the loss is savage. Grief is quick to call and will not leave. Mostly, it stares out at them from the television. They sit in the front room day and night, absorbing whatever is on by osmosis.

They don't notice that Richard and Judy are no longer presenting *This Morning* or that *Coronation Street* has moved out of Weatherfield and is now doing one-off specials. This evening, it's the Platts and the Websters going on a caravan holiday in Derbyshire. On *EastEnders*, the woman who runs the bed-and-breakfast is killed by falling masonry. It seems amazing how often, when you turn on the TV or switch channels, you are confronted by an image of sudden death, which provokes a scramble for the remote.

At intervals, without anyone asking, someone goes off to make tea or sandwiches. The phone rings constantly. Joe wonders how so many journalists have their number. Les never gave interviews to the press. Mostly, the voice says it wants to do 'a tribute to Les', and it will take only five minutes of Elaine's time. She always says no.

Whenever there is a knock on the door, Elaine can feel her heart pounding so hard that it seems to be leaping out of her body, as if she were a character in a Warner Bros. cartoon. She is astonished people can't hear it. At one point, they are confronted on their doorstep by what looks like a teenage girl, who appears to be visibly shaking. She avoids their gaze and tells them she is from the *Daily Mirror.* 'I'm just a trainee. They told me to knock on your door and ask you some questions. I didn't want to knock on your door, but they told me I'd lose my job if I didn't.'

They feel sorry for her, wonder why the *Mirror* hasn't sent a proper reporter with a cigarette dangling in his mouth and a quarter-bottle of whisky in the pocket of his beige mac. Perhaps the *Mirror* has sent her because they assume the family will feel sorry for her, that they will make an exception. But they shake their heads, just like they shake their heads at everyone – even the *Waltham Forest Guardian.*

There is a cemetery behind their old house on Chingford Mount. It is where the Krays are buried. Like Les, the Krays had made the short journey to Chingford from Bethnal Green. One by one they were all buried amid the pine-cone strewn pathways in Chingford Mount, Violet in

1982, Ronnie in 1995, Reggie in 2000. Squirrels now skipped between their headstones.

The saddest was Frances Kray, Reggie's wife. Her brother, Frank Shea, was a driver for the Krays, and in Reggie's words, Frank's sister possessed 'the most beautiful brown eyes I had ever seen'. They were married in April 1965 at St James the Great in Bethnal Green. Ronnie was best man, David Bailey took the photographs, and Diana Dors was among the guests. Frances' mother Elsie wore black as a protest. A little over two years later, Elsie was back at St James the Great, again wearing black, this time for her daughter's funeral. At the epicentre of a violent, passionate marriage, Frances had committed suicide by taking an overdose.

Perhaps Les should have been buried in Chingford Mount, near his old home, near the family that had fascinated him since he first saw their suits and their cars gliding along Vallance Road. However, in February, his nephew Sam had been killed on his motorcycle, struck by a car turning right as he drove on the main road through Epping Forest.

In the days after Les's death, the family would have drinks pressed into their hands by people who knew they barely touched alcohol but who wanted to offer something, anything to help them through the day. Sam's father had come over to Elaine and said: 'You know, when Sam died, people would tell me to have a brandy, have a whisky. "It will help you push your boy to the back of your mind," they said. When I woke up, the first thing in my mind was that I had a hangover. The second thought was that my son was still dead.'

Sam had been buried in the catacombs of the City of London Cemetery, where the long grass and gorse bushes of Wanstead Flats meet the edge of Epping Forest. It was decided that Les's body should be placed in the wall opposite him. The West Ham chaplain, Elwin Cockett, agreed to lead the service. Dressed in full motorcycle leathers, he biked over to Loughton to discuss what he might say at the funeral. Although it is the sole reason for their existence, death is not mentioned often in cemeteries. People 'pass on' or 'pass over'. It seemed every other occupant of Chingford Mount 'fell asleep'. Even George Cornell fell asleep on 9 March 1966, although he did so with a bullet from Reggie Kray's pistol in his head. Les's headstone said 'the sun went down' on him on 19 August 2001. It was a good phrase, one that made him sound like a cowboy out on the range. He would have liked that.

The City of London Cemetery is austerely beautiful. It is entered through a stone arch, its paths patrolled by pink and purple rhododendron bushes. Bobby Moore had been buried here, quietly and privately, in 1993. Only later, when a nation realised what had been lost, would there be something more public: a memorial service at Westminster Abbey.

It might not have been Westminster Abbey, but there was

quite a turnout to say goodbye to Leslie Jesse Sealey, goal-keeper. Sir Alex Ferguson was one of the few managers of his not to attend, but he sent Elaine a letter. So, more unexpectedly, did Jackie Milburn's wife. Milburn was the greatest player Newcastle ever produced; he was also Bobby Charlton's cousin. His goals had contributed to three FA Cups, and his death in October 1988 was marked by what was almost a state funeral on Tyneside. Laura Milburn sent Elaine a postcard, saying she had watched Les play at St James' Park and been struck by not just how well he had performed but how much he had seemed to enjoy the occasion.

Lawrence agreed to take a photograph of West Ham's keepers – Shaka Hislop, Craig Forrest and Stephen Bywater – carrying the coffin. It would be offered to any paper that wanted it. Stephen had been especially affected by Les's death. He'd come down to London from Rochdale as a teenager.

Joe, who had trained with all of them, would have liked to have joined them, but his ruined shoulder would not have stood for it. If he'd tried to carry the coffin, he would have dropped it.

Stephen Bywater did think he might drop it. The weight, as he carried it into the chapel, was excruciating. Once they had laid it down, he went over to Elaine.

'I thought you said Les had lost weight.'

'But he had lost weight. Oh, you did know the coffin's lead-lined, didn't you?'

The Reverend Cockett was more conventionally dressed as the congregation sang the FA Cup final hymn 'Abide with Me'. Like Reggie Kray's funeral in Bethnal Green the year before, the service climaxed with 'My Way'.

Time does not heal grief, at least not at first. The weeks immediately after Les's death were hard, but they were easier than what followed. Grief was like being swept along by a fast-flowing river. There were visitors, cards, phone calls, often from people whose voices you had not heard for years. There were enough flowers to make 22 Hurst Avenue seem like an adjunct of Kew Gardens. There was the funeral to prepare for, readings to learn. Then, at the wake, came the stories, the laughter, the promises to keep in touch.

Gradually, the phone stopped ringing, the knocks on the door began to cease and the flowers in the vases started to wither and fade. Then the river that had carried them along emptied into a still, silent, shipless sea. There, they drifted.

It was the small, often trivial conversations with her husband that Elaine missed, rather than the grand debates as to whether England would win the World Cup in Japan or whether Iain Duncan Smith, who had succeeded Norman Tebbit as Chingford's MP, was the right man to lead the Conservative Party. She wanted to talk to him about the price of a gallon of petrol, what they should have for dinner, how Joe should stop trying so hard to be the man of the family. Sometimes she would hold an imaginary conversation, or rather an imaginary monologue, because Les never answered now. Sometimes Elaine would feel only silence staring back at her. Even months afterwards, there was still the sense of disbelief that this had happened to her. The sense of loneliness persisted, particularly when she was with other people.

She consoled herself with the thought that they had met and married young. Les had been forty-three when he died, so the children were not eight and six but eighteen and sixteen. Elaine would not have to sit them down in the living room, fumble through a drawer and pull out a packet of photographs and say: 'This was your father.'

The river became glassily calm, and the only sound was from a woman and her two boys telling themselves over and over again: 'We are fine.'

Carry on Abroad

I am in Thailand, on the beach at Pattaya. Above me, the sky is a perfect blue. The sand is from a holiday brochure. The Indian Ocean is aquamarine. Coming towards me is a bloke wanting to sell something.

It is May 1981. Coventry have finished sixteenth in the First Division. We have survived another season and are celebrating with a tour of the Far East: Thailand, Malaysia, Hong Kong, Indonesia. By the time we get back, it will practically be time to start pre-season. With me is Peter Bodak, a winger who drives me mad by chipping the ball over me in training, and Stevie Jacobs, the full-back.

This wizened old man comes towards us, stops, looks at us for a long time and says: 'Do you want to buy a diamond?'

Stevie tells him to fuck off. I say: 'No, thanks,' but Peter's eyes are lighting up. 'What diamond?'

The man takes two lumps of wood out from a holdall and produces a diamond from a pouch. It's as big as a car's headlight bulb. He tells us a story, claiming that he is a miner from Borneo and comes to Thailand to sell smuggled, uncut diamonds to tourists.

Straight away, Stevie and I see the problem with his story. Uncut diamonds are dull and milky in colour, not shiny like this one, and a diamond this size would be worth about £8 million. To prove it is a diamond, the guy hits it with a lump of wood. The wood smashes. Peter wants to know how much. He is told $200. Peter knocks him down by $20, and then puts the diamond in his shoe for safety while we sunbathe.

When we get to Bangkok, Peter takes it to a jeweller, and to make sure it is worth even more has it fitted in a ring. The ring costs $200. When it's set, he asks the jeweller how much it's worth now.

'Four hundred,' comes the reply.

'Four hundred grand? As much as that?'

'No, four hundred dollars. The stone is zircon. It's almost worthless.'

Under Jimmy Hill, Coventry were big on overseas trips, on flying the flag. We were pretty naive travellers. When we went to Reykjavik as a favour for the Icelandic FA, I thought the place would have a post office, some reindeer and nothing else. But it was a proper city, full of brightly painted houses, although our behaviour was so bad – one of our number became so drunk he decided to use a rubber plant in the foyer as a urinal – we had to leave our beautiful hotel, ending up in a glorified bed-and-breakfast.

There was a marriage across the way, and the groom thought it would be a real coup to invite the Coventry City team to his wedding reception. His mistake, because we all became very drunk, and a player tried to kiss the bride – and I don't mean a peck on the cheek. The place erupted like a saloon bar in a John Wayne movie. We had ruined their big day. That's British footballers when they're away from home. Booze, booze, booze, and screw the consequences.

There was no booze in Saudi Arabia, but there were some very nice gifts. Jimmy Hill did a lot of work with the Saudi Arabian FA, who paid his company £25 million to develop football in the kingdom (later, he would lose a lot of that money on a football venture in Detroit). It meant we made a few trips to the capital, Riyadh. We attended a banquet that was hosted by Prince Faisal, who was overseeing a project to make Saudi Arabia a force in the world game. After the meal, we went up to be presented to the prince. Before the dinner, Gordon Milne had told us: 'Take the present with your left hand, shake the prince's hand with your right. Then you bow and leave the stage.'

We were each given a box. I thought it would contain a plate, which is the usual thing you are given after this kind of do, or maybe a set of coffee cups, given how much of the stuff they seemed to drink in Riyadh. When we got on the coach, I opened the box and saw it contained a twenty-four-carat solid gold watch with a sun and moon dial. When I got home, I had it valued at £5,000. At the time, you could get a pretty decent house in Coventry for £10,000. They had given us the equivalent of the deposit on a house without even thinking about it or realising how much it was worth to us. They did so with a flick of the wrist.

There wasn't much to do in Riyadh, but I decided to go to the gold market. It's five minutes from the hotel, but the streets are narrow and crowded and I lose my way. I can't imagine a worse place in which to be lost. All the signs are in Arabic, and hardly anybody speaks English. Then I arrive at a wide square called Al Deera. There are hundreds of people milling about; the atmosphere is intense. They seem to be intoxicated. Everyone is talking loudly, excitedly. They can't possibly be drunk because we have had it spelled out to us in very basic language on the plane and in the hotel that you cannot drink alcohol in Saudi Arabia under any circumstances.

Because I am tall, I can see over the heads of most people. Gradually, I make my way to the front. There is a van parked in the square. A boy of about fourteen or fifteen is hauled out and taken to a block. A policeman puts the boy's hand on the block, and someone emerges with a scimitar that looks like it should be in *The Arabian Nights*. It comes swishing down, and the boy's hand is chopped off. He passes out from the pain and is taken away immediately. The crowd cheer and gesticulate wildly. Then a man is bundled out of the van and dragged to the block, his hands tied behind his back. He is knelt down beside the block. The crowd are hysterical by now, punching the air and cheering. It's like they've just scored a goal or won a penalty. The scimitar swishes again, horizontally this time. Blood spurts everywhere and soaks the stones. Apparently, the man was guilty of having sex with his brother's wife, which counts as rape. His body is taken away, to cheers from the crowd. His sister-in-law has already been executed – stoned to death. They don't do it here. Being beheaded is considered an upgrade. It's like something out of *Life of Brian*. Except that it's just happened.

In the season after my debut, 1977/8, I played only three games. Jim Blyth was still number one. Coventry finished seventh, the second-highest position in their history, and Jim was called up by Scotland for the World Cup in Argentina. He didn't play, but unlike Alan Rough, at least his reputation wasn't about to be wrecked by disasters against Peru and Iran.

In 1979, Manchester United offer Coventry £440,000 for Jim. He is about to become the world's most expensive goalkeeper when he fails his medical because of a back injury. He comes back to Highfield Road to dreams that are a little more ordinary.

Until he moved to Birmingham in 1982, Jim would always start the season as number one but never finish it. I would generally have the second half of the season. The trouble with Coventry was they would always sell their best players. You would never go into a season thinking, 'We might make the top five, we might make Europe.'

Coventry's two main strikers then were Mick Ferguson and Ian Wallace – a classic big man/small man partnership. In the summer of 1980, Coventry sold Wallace to Nottingham Forest for £1 million. Brian Clough negotiated the transfer with Wallace while they watched Björn Borg play John McEnroe in the Wimbledon final. Wallace had said he'd wanted to leave Highfield Road because Coventry would never invest in the squad.

Jimmy Hill does invest in the training ground. There will be squash and badminton courts, five-a-side pitches and function and conference rooms. Everything can be hired out. Often, I go up front in the five-a-sides and give a running commentary, until I am told to shut up.

Eight years before Hillsborough, Coventry have an all-seater stadium, although realistically nobody is going to play an FA Cup semi-final at Highfield Road. No sooner had the seats been installed than Leeds fans, watching their side losing 4–0, ripped them up and used them as weapons.

We were also given cars. Okay, we were each given a Talbot Solara. Such was the need to raise cash that Hill negotiated a sponsorship deal with Talbot, whose factory was near our training ground at Ryton. The deal was that our name would be changed from Coventry City to Coventry Talbot. The Football League put a stop to that, but we got to keep the cars.

In 1981, the year we went off to the Far East, Coventry came as near as they had ever done in their history to reaching Wembley. We were twenty-nine minutes away from a League Cup final. We started the run by beating Manchester United home and away, both times 1–0. Jim Blyth plays in those matches. We beat Brighton 2–1, and I'm in the side for the fourth-round tie against Cambridge. It's a dreadful game. Cambridge equalise through Alan Taylor, who had scored for West Ham in the 1975 FA Cup final. If they hadn't hit the post, they would have won.

The replay is at the Abbey Stadium. We are one up and there are twenty-six minutes left when Danny Thomas brings down Tommy O'Neill on the edge of the area. It's outside the box, but it's given as a penalty. Their captain, Steve Spriggs, takes it. He has not missed one all season. While the referee is waiting for everyone to calm down, the Cambridge centre-half, Steve Fallon, tells Mark Hateley that Spriggs will put the penalty to my left because he always does. Mark, who is still only eighteen, signals which way the kick will go. I go to my left and at full stretch tip the shot round the post. The *Coventry Evening Telegraph* calls it the save of my life.

We destroy Watford 5–0 in the quarter-final at Highfield

Road. Peter Bodak scores a spectacular goal; Hateley, whose dad Tony played for Coventry in the 1960s, scores twice. Within the space of four years, he will be transferred to AC Milan.

Coventry will play West Ham for a place in the League Cup final. West Ham might look like underdogs, being a division below us, but they are thoroughbreds – Phil Parkes, Trevor Brooking, Billy Bonds, Frank Lampard, Alan Devonshire. They won the FA Cup last season and played Liverpool in the Charity Shield. That's two trips to Wembley in a single summer. We have never been. Not once. Coventry have never actually made it to a semi-final before. The interest is huge. It is being billed as the biggest game since Coventry beat Wolves to win promotion to the big league in 1967. There were 51,000 at Highfield Road then, there will be nearly as many now. It's on the telly, with Hugh Johns commentating for ITV.

Ten minutes before half-time, West Ham are two up. The goals are as soft as duck down. There's a tame header from Billy Bonds that squeezes under my body. Under my bloody body. I try to grab the ball back, but it slithers over the muddy line. I look up to see if the referee, George Courtney, has noticed, but he has. 0–1. Then Garry Thompson turns with the ball and runs into his own area, trying to shield it from Alan Devonshire. I don't know why our centre-forward should be in his own penalty area, but I come out, screaming: 'Keeper's!' Garry clips it back towards where he imagines I am, but we are alongside each other and the ball is rolling into the net. 0–2. He sinks to his knees and probably expects me to bawl him out. I whisper in his ear: 'I said: "Keeper's."'

By the end of the night, Garry has a hat-trick: one goal in our net, two in theirs. We force West Ham further and further back. With every goal we score, the noise grows. By the end, it's deafening. We have won 3–2. 'Super City Set for Wembley' is the headline in the *Coventry Evening Telegraph*.

Upton Park is seething for the second leg. I don't like crosses, or rather I tend not to come for them – I leave that to the centre-halves, Gary Gillespie and Paul Dyson. Trevor Brooking is in commanding form, and Paul's memory of the semi-final is of me yelling: 'Dys – away!' every time a cross comes in.

Paul Goddard breaks through for West Ham, Garry Thompson has one cleared off the line for Coventry, and then a free kick from Billy Bonds deflects off Gary Gillespie straight into the path of Jimmy Neighbour, who so far has done nothing in the whole match. He has now. Gary will go on to play for Liverpool and Celtic, and he will never forget the noise when Neighbour's shot strikes the net. We have lost 4–3. 'Only the brilliance of Les Sealey kept them in the match at all,' reports Neville Foulger in the *Evening Telegraph*. Quite right.

Mad Hatter

'Fuck off. Fuck off.' The Coventry fans are yelling at me, and I am yelling back at them. It's May 1983, the last day of what has turned out to be a car crash of a season. We are losing 4–2 at home to West Ham, and there are blokes three yards behind my goal who seem to believe I am letting them in deliberately because I have already decided to leave Highfield Road. They are rubbing their fingers together to suggest I've been paid for this game – and not by Coventry City. They can fuck off. You know when they say it's never a conspiracy, it's always a cock-up. I've had four cock-ups in this game, two of them to Tony Cottee.

Gordon Milne, the man who signed me, has gone. He was relieved of his duties not long after we lost the League Cup semi-final to West Ham. Because they didn't have the balls to sack him, they made him 'executive manager'. He was told to sit in an office, while Dave Sexton, who had just been fired by Manchester United, took over the first team. It was a prison with a swivel chair and a desk. Gordon soon escaped.

At the end of December, we'd beaten Manchester United 3–0. We'd been fifth in the First Division, and the *Evening Telegraph* was talking about Coventry playing in Europe, something they had done only once before. In 1970, they had entered the Fairs Cup, gone to Munich and been thrashed by Bayern, 6–1. That had been their European adventure. They thought it was time for another one.

On New Year's Day, we'd gone to Luton and won, 2–1. There was more talk of Europe. Towards the end of a season, when a team is comfortably mid-table, with nothing to play for, and starts tossing off games, the press talks about them being 'on the beach'. We must have been looking at some winter sun brochures because we were on the beach from January. There were twenty games remaining. Coventry won two of them. We escaped relegation only after the penultimate game of the season, at Stoke.

By then, Coventry had sold their main striker, Garry Thompson, to West Brom; Jimmy Hill was leaving, and so too was Dave Sexton. I loved working for Dave. He was a wonderful coach, a step up from Milne, and he might have made a real success of Coventry had he not had the rug pulled from under his feet.

In the summer, Mark Hateley and Gary Gillespie would be

allowed to quit for Portsmouth and Liverpool respectively. This was how Coventry City celebrated its centenary.

I got a call from Milne, who was now at Leicester. He had just got them promoted to the top division. There was also an offer from David Pleat to join Luton. Like Coventry, Luton were a Cinderella club. They had actually come closer to relegation than we had. On the final day of the season, they had gone to Maine Road. Manchester City needed a point to survive. Luton needed a win. They won, and on the final whistle, Pleat had danced on to the pitch.

I spent a long time weighing the offers up. Leicester were the bigger club, and I knew Milne, though I didn't necessarily like him. They had a good forward line: Alan Smith and Gary Lineker. They had the second-best defensive record in the Second Division, and their goalkeeper, Mark Wallington, who had understudied Peter Shilton, had been at Filbert Street forever. But he would be thirty-one in September, and I had five years on him. Luton, in contrast, had conceded eighty-four goals. They played entertaining football and had scored more than Manchester United, although it wouldn't be that entertaining if you were Luton's goalkeeper. No Division One team since Southampton in 1967 had conceded eighty-four goals and survived. Successful teams, no matter how much flair they have, don't tend to ship goals. Not at that rate.

What settled the matter was the fact that if I went to Kenilworth Road, I could go back to living in London and maybe buy a house in Chingford, which was then famous for being Norman Tebbit's constituency. However, I knew that while going to Luton would take me home, it might leave me horribly exposed by their defence. I'd be the convenient scapegoat.

In my first season at Kenilworth Road, I conceded sixty-six goals, which was a 20 per cent reduction on the year before. Luton still attacked, but this time around they didn't have to rely on winning the last game of the season to stay up. I thought I'd done my job, but at first Pleat didn't seem to rate me. He certainly rolled his eyes whenever I bought some shirts, jackets or other gear to the training ground in case the lads wanted a bargain. A 'wheeler-dealer', he called me.

In the summer of 1984, he bought Andy Dibble from Cardiff City and started the new season with him in goal. We were different types of goalkeepers. Andy came for everything. If a cross comes in, I'll stay on my line and leave it to the centre-halves, then clear up any mess. Steve Foster, a central defender who's the new Luton captain now that Brian Horton has gone off to manage Hull, prefers my approach. He knows exactly where he stands.

By November, I was still not playing, but Pleat seemed to have changed his mind about how to play in the First Division. He had brought in Foster from Aston Villa, Peter Nicholas from Crystal Palace as a holding midfielder, and Mick Harford from Birmingham – three people who played in the spine of the team, three people prepared to put their foot in.

Steve keeps telling Pleat that he wants me back in the team. Soon, the captain gets his way. I'm back in, and we are playing Everton for a place in the FA Cup final. We had played Millwall in the quarter-final at Kenilworth Road. The result had been a 1-0 home win. Nobody will remember that game, but they will remember the riots that smashed up the ground. The seats in the away end were ripped up. Millwall fans and some who were just along for the ride had poured on to the pitch. They had hurled billiard balls into the directors' box. The area outside the ground had been smashed to bits. I kept thinking: 'We can't go on. This has to be called off.' But we ploughed on.

In the second half, I'm standing in front of the Millwall fans. We are 1-0 up, and the thought occurs to me that they are going to break through the thin line of police and stewards and stop the match. I feel something hard crack against my shoulder. Every few minutes there's a missile thrown. One of them glints in the floodlights and a knife lands in the goalmouth. With a six-inch blade.

Eventually, the referee shouts: 'Les, the moment the ball is kicked up the other end, I am going to blow for full-time, so get ready to run.' And we do, some of us faster than at any point in the entire quarter-final. The Millwall fans pour on to the pitch again. There are coins, stones and bits of bloody masonry flying through the air. A policeman is hit by a brick and has to be given mouth-to-mouth resuscitation.

David Pleat and the chairman, David Evans, who rather embarrassingly is standing to become an MP at the next election – as a Conservative candidate – are summoned to meet Mrs Thatcher. They are told that less than twenty years after Bobby Moore had held up the World Cup, football is in the gutter. We are in the gutter. People are ashamed of us, and that shame is only going to grow, because a couple of months later, the main stand at Bradford City, which is made of wood and filled with hidden rubbish, will burn down. Fifty-six dead. The season will finish off with Liverpool fans running amok at the European Cup final in Brussels. Thirty-nine dead.

The answer is electric fences, membership schemes, no away fans. Less than a week after Luton play Nottingham Forest in the 1989 League Cup final comes Hillsborough. And if we were in the gutter in 1985, then where are we now?

Millwall did not pay a penny for the wreckage their fans caused: their £7,500 fine was overturned on appeal. They paid in other ways, though. When the Docklands Light Railway was being expanded across the Isle of Dogs, they were going to call the station 'Millwall'. They changed their minds, calling it 'Mudchute' instead.

Our reward for beating them is a semi-final against Everton, the most successful side in the country. They are competing for a treble. They are playing Bayern Munich in the semi-finals of the Cup Winners' Cup and have lost just one of their last twenty-four matches. They are top of the First Division, while Luton are fourth bottom, out of the relegation zone on goal difference.

With four minutes to go at Villa Park, Luton are 1–0 up. Kevin Sheedy takes a free kick. It squeezes round the wall and inside the far post. It's extra time. Andy Gray puts Peter Reid through on goal, and I make the save. Then comes another free kick, four minutes from the end of extra time, and Derek Mountfield heads it home. Everton, not Luton, will play Manchester United at Wembley.

Looking back, I don't feel that pain of losing. In 1985, Everton were probably the best side in Europe. They would win the First Division by a mile and would beat Bayern Munich to reach the Cup Winners' Cup final. They would win it in Rotterdam and lose the FA Cup final only in extra time. No, Luton did well, very well to have stretched Everton that far. To near breaking point.

Ghosts

This is a true story. Well, of course it is. I wouldn't be telling it otherwise. But I do need you to believe me.

David Pleat was the kind of manager who liked to take his players away before big games. Not to Majorca or to play golf at La Manga, but to country-house hotels. He particularly liked Henlow Grange, a spa attached to a Georgian manor house built on the site of a monastery in Bedfordshire. It was not far from the London Road, heading north.

It's March 1986. Luton have made the quarter-finals of the FA Cup by beating Arsenal after two replays. This means we have three days to prepare for the biggest match of our season, against Everton, who are five points clear at the top of Division One, with a game in hand.

I always asked to room on my own. That's partly because I like to watch telly until late at night. It's also because we are away on business. If you're an accountant, you don't share a hotel room with another accountant so you can build up a bit of team spirit before going through the books of the local construction company in the morning.

The hotel had a modern extension, which was where all the double rooms were. I was the only one in the old part of the house, in room nine. When you approach it, you walk down five steps and then open the door. Another nine or ten steps take you into the bedroom itself. The stairs outside the door creak. To your left is the bed. If you are lying in it and turn your head at a right angle, you can see the stairs leading into the room. The television is at the bottom of the bed, and the window is behind the TV.

After dinner, I was lying in bed watching a film starring Lee Marvin called *The Big Red One*. It's a war picture about a soldier leading his men through North Africa and Normandy, who is haunted by the fact that in the First World War he had killed a German soldier after the Armistice was declared. When it was over, I turned the telly off, brushed my teeth and went to sleep. I shut the bathroom door. I am certain about that. I definitely shut the bathroom door. I turned the lights off.

I always sleep with the curtains open, and I do so naked. There was a half-moon shining through the window, with more light provided by the security lamp that was directed down at the car park below. I heard the stairs creak outside. Then there was the sound of someone walking down the steps to my door. 'It must be someone going to the wrong room,' I thought, but now there were footsteps on my side of the door. I turned my head, and there, two steps from the bottom, was a man of perhaps forty or fifty years of age. He was dressed as a footman. His body was not blurred or hazy but bathed in a kind of light. He was wearing a three-cornered hat, a shirt with large, billowing, buttoned-up sleeves, trousers that reached his knees and stockings. His shoes were big and clumpy. He turned and looked at me. Straight at me. My sweat began soaking the sheets. Then I wet the bed. I wet the bloody bed. He looked right through me, walked across the room and through the bathroom door.

I pulled off the sheets, ran out of the room and went down to the hotel reception. It was only then that I realised I had no clothes on. The hotel bar was by the reception, and it hadn't closed. There were people walking towards me, going back to their rooms.

The night porter came rushing out of his office, flung a towel around my waist and dragged me into the kitchens. It was like something out of *Fawlty Towers*.

'What the hell are you doing? Have you locked yourself out of your room, sir?'

I told him what I'd seen.

'Well, what do you want me to do about it?'

'I want you to get me another fucking room. I am not staying in that room tonight.'

'Are you drunk?'

'No, I hardly touch the stuff. I'm a professional footballer.' I didn't tell him I'd wet the bed. That would not have advanced my argument.

Then a second night porter appeared, younger than the first. He went with me up to the room. It was empty.

'I'm still not staying. I want another room.'

'The hotel's fully booked, sir.'

We argued. I pleaded in a way I had never done before, until he said: 'There's sort of a room where I can put you up.'

The only thing they had was a room in the new part of the hotel which they used for storage. There were beds piled up against the wall. I pulled a single bed down and found some sheets; there were no blankets. I grabbed some pillowcases and tried to go to sleep.

The following morning, the duty manager knocked on the door. 'Excuse me, sir, but I've heard what happened last night. Have you told anybody about what you think you saw?'

I told him I saw a man dressed as if he were from the eighteenth century come into my room, look at me and walk straight through the bathroom door.

He said: 'I would appreciate you not saying anything about it.'

'Don't you believe me then?'

'It's not for me to say whether I believe you or not. What I can tell you is that someone has had a similar experience in this hotel before. In your room, as it happens. It was one of our staff. In housekeeping. She was making a bed up when a man wearing a three-cornered hat walked into the room and through the bathroom door. She packed in her job that morning.'

He told me that room nine used to be part of a corridor that led towards the grand bedrooms of the house, where the owners and their guests slept. Footmen would carry food and drink from the kitchens along that corridor. Apparently, they still did.

I don't mention this to anyone at breakfast. I certainly don't tell David Pleat, who has organised the trip so that we are properly rested, that his goalkeeper has spent the night in a storage room. I gulp down coffees to try to keep my thoughts about last night at bay. When the physio, John Sheridan, remarks that I look a little clammy and asks if I'm all right, I just nod and say I'm fine. I can't look John in the eye and say: 'Well, since you ask, I had this confrontation with a footman from the eighteenth century last night. I'm just wondering if you can give me anything for that?'

Like the night before, the afternoon is about confronting ghosts. The week leading up to it had been full of conversations about how last season Everton had squeezed past us to reach Wembley. But once the match begins, I calm down, dissolving into the game, and when Mark Stein runs through to score our second, I think that if we keep our nerves and our concentration, Luton will be going through to a second straight FA Cup semi-final.

With twenty-five minutes remaining at Kenilworth Road, we are two goals up against the best team in the country. We manage to hold out for two minutes. Just like at Villa Park, it's a free kick that earns Everton their breakthrough. Pat Van den Hauwe takes it, and this time it's Graeme Sharp heading in. I don't move, stranded on my line.

We try to hold on, but we are creaking and cracking. Then Gary Lineker's bicycle kick rebounds off Steve Foster's chest, straight into the path of Adrian Heath. It's 2–2. When I watch the tie again on *Match of the Day*, I am struck by how pale I look.

The replay is at Goodison Park. Since he left Leicester for Everton, Lineker's game has changed. He scores more with his head, he breaks from deeper, he takes on defenders and he is astonishingly quick. After a quarter of an hour, he does it again, sprinting past Steve and into the penalty area. Naturally, he scores. It's his thirty-third of the season, and we are only in March.

Before half-time, he breaks through again, and I bring him down as he powers towards goal. Lineker is just too fast. Trevor Steven takes a not particularly good penalty, and I save it comfortably, going to my left. A goalkeeper who saves a penalty is routinely described as a hero. Headlines on the back page are guaranteed – with one proviso: his team has to win. Although Mark Stein strikes the post, Luton don't.

Deep in the night, as the coach makes the journey down

the M6 and on to the M1 past the familiar service stations – Sandbach, Hilton Park, Newport Pagnell – I wonder
if I will ever make it to an FA Cup final. You don't get too
many opportunities at a little club like Luton, and we have
already had two good shots at it. We missed both times.
Not by much, but we missed.

By now Lawrence Lustig was doing a lot of work in boxing,
which is a sport I've always loved. Where I grew up in
Bethnal Green was near enough to York Hall that you
could smell the liniment, the sweat and the Turkish baths,
which is what the hall was originally designed for before
boxing came along.

Lawrence had got to know Barry McGuigan, and one
day he asked if I fancied coming to watch him train at the
Vauxhall Sports Club. Everything in Luton appears to have
some connection with Vauxhall. It's as much a company
town as Dagenham is with Ford. I am actually trying my
hand at selling Vauxhalls. There's a car lot over the way
from the ground, and I am helping out the guy who runs
it. Lawrence had taken a photo of me dressed as Arthur
Daley, complete with sheepskin jacket, trilby and cigar,
leaning on some old banger.

I watch McGuigan and, frankly, I am not all that
impressed. He does some stretches, a few circuits and some
gentle punching of the bag. Then he stops. McGuigan had
lost his world title in the desert heat of Las Vegas. The

whole country had watched him on telly as he collapsed, exhausted and dehydrated, on to the canvas. It was horrible. Perhaps he had scaled down his routine now, not wanting to drive himself too hard. It's understandable.

'I expected more than this,' I whisper to Lawrence. Then I go over to Barry and say: 'Is that all you do nowadays?'

McGuigan looks straight at me: 'That's my warm-up.'

Then he launches into some rhythmic pad work with his trainer, before going back to the bag, this time pummelling it furiously. This is followed up by a full-scale sparring session, which lasts for what seems like a couple of hours. He finishes drowned in sweat. As we leave, I say to Lawrence: 'I don't expend that much energy in a week.'

David Pleat had left to take over at Tottenham. John Moore, who had run Luton's reserve team, had been promoted upwards. He lasted just one season before resigning. Moore didn't like the pressure, didn't like being front of stage. Luton had, nevertheless, just finished seventh, the highest position in their history. For a club of Luton's size and resources, it was a tremendous achievement. Our average gate at Kenilworth Road was 10,000, the second lowest in the league. Only Wimbledon drew fewer.

We were committed. There was a real togetherness about Luton Town. We also had the advantage of playing on a plastic pitch. Queens Park Rangers had installed AstroTurf at Loftus Road in 1981. So had Oldham and Preston. I didn't like it. I thought AstroTurf was good for hockey or tennis, where the true bounce of a ball is essential. In football it was okay as a training surface, but if you weren't used to it, it was difficult to play a proper game on AstroTurf. Luton were used to it. Teams who tried to kick the ball long would come to grief at Kenilworth Road. The ball would run on ahead of you and often go out of play. Most teams didn't have players who could cope with it. Only a few teams regularly gave us trouble: teams like Nottingham Forest or Oxford, who would pass the ball to feet.

In 1986/7, we lost only two games at home – to Watford and Oxford. We beat Everton, Liverpool and Tottenham, who made up the top three in the league. The plastic pitch transformed our home record, but the wins also gave us the confidence to play well away from home.

The one thing AstroTurf did was knacker your knees. If you twisted and turned on the plastic, which didn't have the give of grass, it could cause you problems. Alex Ferguson wanted to bring Mick Harford to Manchester United in 1992. The pitch at Old Trafford was terrible, and he thought they could whack the ball long and Mick would be able to elbow the centre-halves out of the way. But he failed the medical on account of his knees. Ferguson remained convinced that had the deal gone through, United rather than Leeds would have won the league that season. I survived because I always wore padded tracksuit bottoms. The only goalkeeper who wore shorts on the plastic was Everton's Neville Southall.

Moore was replaced by his assistant, Ray Harford. In his first season we reached two cup finals. The first was the Simod Cup, which was a piece of nothing. It was supposed to replace the European games that English football had lost after the Heysel ban, although the teams who were most likely to have played in Europe – Arsenal, Liverpool, Manchester United and Tottenham – did not take part in it.* We ended up playing Reading in the final. The game was a fiasco, and we were thrashed 4–1. I can't explain the result. Mick Harford punched the ball into the net – something the referee didn't notice – to give us the lead, but we then fell apart against a team that got itself relegated to Division Three at the end of the season.

A month later, at the same venue, Wembley, came the greatest day in the history of Luton Town: the 1988 League Cup final. I should have been part of it. I'd been inspired when we beat Ipswich in the last sixteen – 'Luton Win a Tribute to Sealey' was the headline in *The Times,* the paper of record – and I had been pretty much untroubled when we beat Oxford in the semis. Then came a freezing Tuesday-night league game at home to Sheffield Wednesday. I come for a cross. It's something I usually leave to the centre-halves, but there's no choice. Lee Chapman is barrelling

---

* In May 1985, thirty-nine, mainly Italian, fans were killed in rioting before the European Cup final between Liverpool and Juventus. As a result, all English clubs were banned from European football for five years. Liverpool's punishment was extended by an additional year.

towards me, and we collide. Violently. I hit the AstroTurf and my shoulder goes. It takes six minutes of treatment before I'm ready to resume. In the end, I can't carry on, and Andy Dibble takes over.

We are then knocked out of the FA Cup by Wimbledon and go down 3–0 to Manchester United at Old Trafford. All the while I am trying to get fit for the League Cup final. I test the shoulder, work on it, plead with it, but I am not fit. Andy will be in goal for a match Arsenal, the holders, are expected to win.

There are some questions I am sure you will want answered. As we travel down to London, knowing I won't be part of things, do I want Luton to win? Absolutely. Do I want Andy to play well? Of course I do – he's a good lad. Do I want Andy to be the hero of the greatest game Luton Town have ever played? I'll have to take the Fifth Amendment on that, because after today Luton will have a new first-choice keeper. You want the people who replace you to succeed, but you don't want to be blotted out of history. If you ask Geoff Hurst if he wants England to win the World Cup again, he'll reply that of course he does. Does he want someone else to score a hat-trick in the final? Not really.

Arsenal are 2–1 up, with time running out, when they are awarded a penalty for a trip on David Rocastle. Nigel Winterburn, who I don't think has ever taken a penalty in his life and has scored just once for Arsenal, volunteers to step up and win the cup. I have no idea why. If you listen to

Brian Moore's commentary, you will hear him say: 'Curious decision, this,' as Winterburn steps up.

It certainly is. Andy saves it low to his left. In the last few minutes, Danny Wilson and Brian Stein score, and, astonishingly, we have won 3–2. It is the first major trophy in Luton's history. Andy is voted man of the match.

That might have been the end of my time at Luton. Certainly, it would have been the end of my time as first-choice keeper. Andy is undroppable now, but in the summer he accepts an offer to join Manchester City, who are a division below Luton but a bigger club. They win promotion the following season. At Kenilworth Road, I am back as number one. That will change, though, after Luton's next trip to Wembley

Not only did Luton win the 1988 League Cup, they made the final the following year. En route we beat Manchester City – with Andy in goal – before facing West Ham in the semi-final. We won the first leg, at Kenilworth Road, 3–0. Roy Wegerle, whose career had taken him from South Africa to Florida and then Chelsea, scored twice for us. One was from a long kick upfield from me; the other came after he was wrestled to the ground by Julian Dicks, who was playing his usual unsophisticated game, and won a penalty.

The second leg, at Upton Park, should have been an irrelevance, but one evening, when I was out of the house, Elaine received a phone call. It was an East End voice.

'Is Les there?'

'No, he's out. Who's speaking?'

'Let's just say, Mrs Sealey, that if Les doesn't start throwing in some goals at West Ham, you might not recognise him when you next see him. You don't live far from us, do you, love? Chingford. Hurst Avenue. You both need to be very careful.'

When I got in, Elaine was distraught. She kept saying: 'I can't believe they've got our number. We're ex-directory.'

The phone rang again. It was the same patter, the same threats. I put it down without speaking and phoned the police. I didn't expect them to do very much. I thought they might just log the call, but they sent someone round who interviewed us and said we should leave the house until the semi-final was over.

We told Joe and George that we were going for a little break and checked into the Marriott at Waltham Abbey. They were five and three and thought it was a bit of an adventure, especially since the Marriott had a pool. The police kept watch on the house, and a plain-clothes copper was sent to the dressing room, sitting next to me while Ray Harford gave his team talk. The policeman walked out with me into the usual vicious atmosphere and then peeled away into the stands.

We won 2–0. West Ham would be relegated a couple of months later. They have been my team since boyhood in Bethnal Green, but this time I wasn't too bothered about what happened to them. We will play Nottingham Forest in the final. They were very lucky to win their semi against Bristol City, who are in the Third Division, and although Forest have all the celebrity that surrounds Brian Clough, we are confident.

We have a pre-Wembley training session, and Lawrence is there with his camera to record it. We practise set pieces, and Ray Harford tells me to stay on my line for a corner. I do, and Mick Harford, who is no relation to the manager but is six foot three and built like a tank, heads it in.

'Where was the challenge?' Ray shouts at me. 'Why didn't you bloody come for it?'

'Because you told me to stay on my fucking line.'

The accusations fly like bits of lead from a shotgun. And then suddenly, in front of a photographer from a tabloid newspaper, the manager of the League Cup holders and his goalkeeper are wrestling with each other. Then we hear Mick's voice, which sounds like a Durham miner's, telling us to stop this nonsense. Eventually, he pulls us apart. We stare at each other. Lawrence does not alert the *Daily Star*, as he probably should have done.

A few days later, inside the dressing room at Wembley, Ray and I are staring at each other once more. The 1989 League Cup final has just finished. We have lost 3–1, and Ray is yelling at me, blaming me for the defeat. I am yelling back, telling him I will never play for him again.

In his commentary for ITV, Brian Moore had described Luton as underdogs. We don't play like underdogs. We play like who we are: the cup holders. Ashley Grimes nearly scores, Mick heads in the opening goal, and Brian Laws clears off the line for Forest. And then Steve Hodge runs into the left side of the area, chased by Steve Foster. This time, I do come off my line. Far too far. I dive at Hodge's feet, and he goes over. It's a penalty. A stupid penalty, because Hodge was still a way from loosing off a shot. It's a mistake, and when you make a mistake as a goalkeeper you tend to pay for it. Nigel Clough scores the penalty, and Luton are no longer the better team. Neil Webb scores the second and then Clough clips one into the very far corner of the net. It's done.

In the dressing room, I tell Ray that I accept the mistake for the penalty, but we lost 3–1; there was still most of the second half to go when Forest equalised. That's when I told him I would never play for him again. I did it in front of the whole dressing room. That was me pretty much finished at Luton Town.

A Small Family Business

There had been two deaths in Joe Sealey's life. There had been his father's, sudden, brutal and final. Then there had been the death of his career. Equally sudden, equally brutal, equally final. They had happened within weeks of each other.

He was a goalkeeper, like his father. He wanted to be nothing else. As soon as Joe was old enough to be properly judged, he was sent to be assessed at Southampton, Sheffield Wednesday, Southend United and West Ham United. Les would have preferred him to have gone to Southend. It was a relentlessly unglamorous club whose stands were fashioned from curved, corrugated iron. For an ambitious teenaged goalkeeper, the fact that Southend would never be part of any Premier League should have been an advantage. 'It won't be nice, it won't be pretty, but you'll play sooner than you would anywhere else,' his father would tell him. 'Go down the divisions and play early. There are four thousand young people like you, and of them only one will make it. You have to live the game, you have to breathe it, eat it and want it every day of your career.'

He did not want Joe around him. Football is a hard, cruel business, and he didn't particularly want to witness that harshness and cruelty being inflicted on his own son. Joe, however, wanted to be at home. He wanted to be with his father, so he chose West Ham, where his father happened to be the goalkeeping coach. They would train at Chadwell Heath. The club had the air of a small family business about it. Harry Redknapp was in charge; his brother-in-law, Frank Lampard, was his number two. Frank coached his own son, whom he had named after himself and whom he was determined would be a better footballer than he was. Since Frank Sr had won the FA Cup twice, the bar was set incredibly high.

Every day, when nobody was around but his father, Frank Jr would be doing something different. He might be in the gym, honing his footwork; he might be out on the pitch, taking penalties; or he might be stretching his stamina with runs around Chadwell Heath. When he had first arrived at West Ham, Joe had thought him ordinary. Then, session by session, he watched as young Frank forced himself to become a proper player. Always there would be the voice of Frank Sr, prodding, pushing, demanding. The tone was cold and insistent. Watching them, Joe didn't quite know why Frank took it. Didn't quite know why he didn't break into pieces or turn on his father, either here or in the car back home to Romford.

As Frank's body hardened and lost its soft edges, so did his mind, but even when he broke into the West Ham first team, he would glance across to the bench at Upton Park during a game, searching not for any instructions relayed by Uncle Harry, but for his father's nod of approval.

Because of his time at Manchester United and Aston Villa, Les had often been an infrequent presence in Joe's life. Perhaps this was why Joe sometimes felt afraid of him. Les never struck him, never grabbed him by the lapels, never threatened him. Yet, even when he was eighteen, Joe would still ask him for permission to go to the cinema. Les had an aura, an inner strength about him, the kind needed to marshal a defence at Manchester United. Occasionally, he would shout at Joe in the same way he screamed at Gary Pallister or Steve Bruce if he caught them out of position, mouth open, head shaking, fingers pointing. He would apologise to Joe more quickly than he had done to his teammates in the dressing room at Old Trafford.

They were living in Loughton now, fifteen minutes from Chadwell Heath. There were several cars parked on the driveway, but Les was adamant he would not be giving his son a lift in any of them. When Joe asked why, Les replied: 'Two reasons. One, under no circumstances is anybody at that club going to see you getting special treatment.'

'What's the other one?'

'You're in at half-eight. I'm due in at half-nine. I'm not spending an extra hour down there just to please you.'

Carrying his kit, Joe would take a bus to Loughton station, a train to Stratford, followed by a connection to Chadwell Heath. He would then walk a mile to the ground. If he was running late, two cars – one driven by Les, the other by Elaine, with Joe in the passenger seat – would leave the house at the same time, bound for the same destination. As he walked through the narrow, shabby entrance, Joe would sometimes see his father arrive, who would give him a wave and a toot of the horn.

After training, Joe and the other keepers would remain behind to practise goal kicks. It was something Les put a high value on, and if a kick did not go beyond the halfway line, there would be words. He would also tell his charges: 'The best goalkeeper is the one who makes the fewest saves because he's the one who controls his area.'

His father's boots were among the five pairs Joe was required to clean every day. One Friday night, Les decided to go off and supervise a youth team game. The rain pelted down. Joe had already gone home. The next day, West Ham were playing at Upton Park. Joe was in the stands when suddenly he received a message to go down to the dressing room. The first team were there, and so was his father, holding up the mud-encased boots like a couple of dead rats. Les launched into his son in front of the men, who to a teenager appeared like gods in tracksuits. He threw the boots at Joe and told him to get out.

Most of the bollockings were delivered not by Les but by Tony Carr, who had been in charge of West Ham's academy since 1973. He had been an apprentice once, and the boots he had cleaned had belonged to Moore, Hurst and Peters. He had not made it at West Ham and, apart from a few matches at Barnet, had not made it anywhere. He knew how hard football was, how sharp its edges could be.

Joe thought Carr could sometimes be a hard, ruthless bastard. So did Rio Ferdinand, Joe Cole, Frank Lampard, Jermain Defoe, Glen Johnson and Michael Carrick. And so did the boys who had won the 1999 FA Youth Cup, thrashing Coventry 9–0 on aggregate. Carr made the board at Upton Park £80 million in transfer fees, and when he left the club in 2016, he was given a severance payment of £14,000, which worked out at £325 for every year of service. That was the West Ham way. Even by the measures of the Premier League it was a hard club. Its catchment area – the East End, the vast council estates of Harold Hill, the tower blocks of Peckham – meant it could not be anything else.

There was a part of Joe that was actually relieved when Les was sacked. Having his father at the club had been one of the main reasons he had joined West Ham, but now it was becoming oppressive. The sackings came in May 2001. They came as a surprise to Harry Redknapp, but not to many of his players, even those as far away from the first team as the teenaged Joe Sealey.

Rio Ferdinand had been sold to Leeds the previous November, partly because the club believed that the Bosman ruling, which meant footballers could leave for nothing if they were out of contract, would make transfer fees obsolete. The chairman, Terry Brown, thought the £18 million Leeds were offering was the kind of money that would soon disappear, so he took it. Redknapp spent some of the money on Svetoslav Todorov, Rigobert Song and Titi Camara. All were dreadful. West Ham finished fifteenth. The players were waiting for the wires to snap, and when Redknapp criticised Brown in print, they did.

Redknapp was shocked. So were the Lampards, although Frank Sr took it better than his son. Beneath the East End camaraderie and the choruses of 'I'm Forever Blowing Bubbles', a song about embracing disappointment, there was a vicious streak among the crowd at Upton Park. They thought Frank was playing only because of who he was rather than what he was. There was a boy who sat behind the home dugout who abused him every time he warmed up. Frank would go into a bank not far from the ground and would always chat to one of the tellers. One day, she introduced Frank to her son. It was the same boy. Lampard left for Chelsea.

Les was rather more sanguine about it all. He had been totally committed to Redknapp and the Lampards.

Redknapp was replaced by Glenn Roeder, who had been number four in his backroom team. Les's job as goalkeeping coach was taken by Luděk Mikloško, a Czech international who had played more than three hundred times for West Ham and whose finest hour had come at Upton Park in May 1995, when he had almost single-handedly kept Manchester United at bay and denied them the league title. Joe found Mikloško more relaxed than his father had been. He felt he had some breathing space now.

Roeder called the squad into the gym and gave the usual address of a new manager. Everyone would have a clean slate. The past would not be held against them.

The next day, Shaka Hislop, West Ham's first-choice keeper under Redknapp, came into the dressing room to discover that the number on the back of his shirt had changed from '1' to '13'. David James, brought in from Aston Villa, was now first choice. Some slates were cleaner than others.

James did not want to train alongside the other goalkeepers, which had always been the way under Redknapp. The reserves and the academy were moved away from Chadwell Heath to Rush Green, which was owned by Ford and was where the company's works teams played. There had long been deep ties between Ford and West Ham. The Ford plant at Dagenham was once a Detroit-on-the-Thames that employed 40,000 and rolled out the Zephyr, the Anglia and the Cortina. Many of its workers could be found at Upton Park watching Moore, Peters and Hurst. It was diminished now, producing only the Fiesta, but its sports pitches were still superb.

Joe disliked David James. James didn't want the young players near him. He had that arrogance, that separateness that comes with being an England international. To Joe, James was the finest natural goalkeeper he had ever seen, but his training was lackadaisical, sloppy. Then, suddenly, he would change gear. Joe watched as he practised dealing with a back pass, something the keepers had never done under Harry. James took the pass and delivered a seventy-yard kick straight to the feet of his man. Everyone looked at him, astonished.

One morning, a couple of years before, Joe had woken up and felt a pain in his neck. There was a part of him that thought he should give training a miss, but West Ham had another goalkeeper of Joe's age who had suffered a serious knee injury, and there was a part of Joe that was quietly pleased that Billy McMahon, a young Dubliner, was out. He would have the stage to himself. The French had a saying: 'The absent are always wrong.' It applied to goalkeepers more than anyone else in football. If you did not play, you were a ghost.

Joe trained. They were testing his reactions, hitting a ball against a wall and seeing how quickly he responded.

He went down and felt his shoulder go. It was dislocated. A physio was called over and put the shoulder back in its socket.

Joe was out for six weeks. They crawled by. Whenever Geoff Boycott was injured, he would stare at the score-card in the *Yorkshire Post* or watch from the pavilion at Headingley and complain that someone else was scoring 'my runs'. That's how goalkeepers felt. That's how Joe felt. Someone else was making his saves.

He returned to fitness. West Ham reserves would be playing Arsenal. It was a big game. People would be watching. In training, his positioning had been good, his reactions sharp; he could sense the swerve or spin on the ball. He was in form. Craig Forrest, West Ham's Canadian reserve keeper, was watching him as he tipped a ball over the bar. There were ten minutes left, ten minutes in which Joe might have wound down, relaxed, but he kept pushing himself. Then came a shot, low to his right. He saved it, full length. Once more, he felt his shoulder go. This time it could not be jammed back into its socket. The arm hung limply and forlornly, pain and frustration flowing through him.

They strapped up the top of his body to restrict the shoulder's movement, and when the strapping was taken off several weeks later, he could barely extend his arm to ninety degrees and was unable to raise it above his head. He was a goalkeeper – a goalkeeper who couldn't move one of his bloody arms.

They offered him something called a rotator-cuff operation, which sounded gentle but wasn't. The tendon that attached the muscle in his shoulder to the bone at the top of his arm, the humerus, was torn. It could not repair itself because there were no longer enough blood capillaries feeding the muscle. Eventually, the tendon would wither and die.

The surgeons cut into the shoulder and drilled holes into the bone. Plastic plugs were inserted into them, and the tendon was stretched over the plugs and reattached. The procedure took six hours. It cost him his first full season at West Ham, who employed a masseur once used by Frank Bruno to push and knead the muscles in his upper body with a force that would reduce Joe to tears. The shoulder was encased in a body suit, which could come off only for showers.

The stitches became infected, and poison began dripping from the wound. Eventually, the poison was drained, the massaging stopped and the body suit came off. He was a footballer once more. His father was no longer in charge of the goalkeepers. This was a chance to be his own man.

The operation had been a success, but it came with a warning: if Joe's shoulder went again, the operation could not be redone. He would never be able to use his arm properly again. There are some warnings that stalk you silently through life, only tapping on your window when they have long been forgotten. This one never left the room, and it confronted him within weeks of his recovery.

There was another training session. A routine shot, a routine save, his hand over the ball. Then there was the same feeling of something giving way in his upper arm. Joe was taken to Holly House, a private hospital in Buckhurst Hill that looked like an Edwardian manor house. As he waited for the X-rays, a thought confronted him: 'I am finished, and I am eighteen years old.'

Then the double doors opened, and he was face to face with his parents. Joe burst into tears. He would never play for West Ham again.

Dinner for One

I am in a hotel, the Ramada in Manchester, not far from Piccadilly station. A lovely two-room suite. It is January 1990, and I am a Manchester United player. On loan. For a month. Paul Ince and Danny Wallace are also in the hotel. I am going down to dinner. It's on the club account. I order four courses.

I have put on a stone and a half since the League Cup final. If Alex Ferguson knew how unfit I was, he would never have asked me to come on loan as cover for Jim Leighton. Having dinner by yourself gives you plenty of time to think, especially if you've ordered four courses. I am thirty-two. I have been playing top-flight football for twelve years and have completely lost my way in the game.

I spent the early part of the season playing for Luton reserves. On the training ground at Vauxhall Motors, I just went through the motions. You know what it's like when you lose interest in a job, and I had lost interest in Luton Town. Luton hadn't won a game in two months, but I refused to play for the first team. Ray Harford asked me point-blank three times to play, and each time I said no. He came to realise that there was no point in wanting someone whose heart wasn't in it to play and stopped asking. I still had two years of a pretty lucrative contract to run.

Stoke had offered £75,000 for me, but Harford told their manager, Mick Mills, that he wanted double that, and the deal fell through. Given how much we both wanted me to leave and that I was still being paid by Luton, he ought to have accepted £7.50 to let me go. Given the state of my body and mind, 75p might have been a more accurate reflection of my worth.

When I go into training, I don't linger and I don't mix with anyone. I go in and go home. I have piled on weight. I am divorced – and not just from the club. I have lost interest in football completely.

I get home late one January night after a reserve team game. Elaine tells me that Harford has been on the phone. 'He wants you to call him back as soon as you arrive.'

I'm intrigued. Harford and I haven't exchanged a dozen words since he last asked me to play for the first team – against Crystal Palace in November. When I call him back, he says that Manchester United would like to take me on a month's loan. Their reserve keeper, Gary Walsh, is injured.

Initially, Fraser Digby had been called in as cover, but he has had to go back to Swindon.

There are two reasons for Harford to be keen on the deal. One, he would get rid of me for a month. He also wants Manchester United to loan him Mal Donaghy, who had spent ten years at Luton as a centre-half but had gone to Old Trafford for £650,000 after the 1988 League Cup final win. It was a lot of money for Alex Ferguson to pay for a thirty-one-year-old centre-half, and the move hadn't really worked out, but Mal is still a good player and Luton's defence badly needs shoring up. We are in the relegation zone.

Knowing how much Harford wants the deal to go through, I decide to screw it up for him. Deliberately. I do it out of pure spite. I just want to make life difficult for him.

I go into his office. He is sat on his swivel chair. When he hears what I have to say – 'No, I don't think I'll go' – he nearly falls off it. It is Thursday morning. If Harford wants Mal Donaghy to play in his team on Saturday, he has until 5pm today to register the loan move. He keeps asking why I don't want to go to a club like Manchester United, and I keep on repeating that I just don't. It is petulant, teenage stuff, and in the end Harford turns to the Luton secretary, Bill Tomlins, and says: 'I am going to training. Sort him out.'

I have a lot of time for Bill. He's a man whom all the players like. He and I talk the situation over. He finishes by saying: 'Do yourself a favour and go. There is nothing for you at Luton, and it won't do you any harm to give Alex Ferguson a ring.'

When he picks up the phone, Ferguson asks how I'm doing and invites me up to Manchester for a month. I agree, but when I ring off, I'm wondering if I've done the right thing. There's a definite fear when I travel north.

Manchester United are doing almost as badly as Luton. They are fifteenth, two points off a relegation place. There is a lot of tension around the place. Paul Ince and Danny Wallace meet me in the foyer and take me to the training ground, the Cliff in Salford. There, everything is laid out for me: shirts, boots, socks – all the kit I would need for a month at United, neatly pressed and folded. At Coventry or Luton, I would have had to search for the stuff in the kit bin. The shirt is a tighter fit than they anticipated, and when the players and management see how much I've gone to seed, they look at me with disgust.

We play a five-a-side, watched by a crowd of five hundred people. Their eyes are on to me immediately. This is the first thing I've noticed about Manchester United: wherever you go, whatever you do, there is pressure, hanging off your shoulders like an ill-fitting suit. Down on the ground, making a save, I look like a beached whale. I'm not remotely fit enough for football at the top level. The United players start calling me 'Cat'. Their voices are laced with sarcasm, but the name will stick.

Ferguson's assistant is Archie Knox, who'd been his

number two through the glory years at Aberdeen. He takes me aside and tells me, bluntly, that if they had known how fat I was, they would never have taken me.

My first assignment is to travel with the team to the City Ground, where they will play Nottingham Forest in the third round of the FA Cup. It's live on the BBC. In the studio, Jimmy Hill is saying United look beaten in the warm-up and that he expects Ferguson to be sacked if they lose.

They win, 1–0. They didn't deserve it. Afterwards, in the tunnel, I meet Tony Gubba, who is wearing a leather coat that makes him look like a Luftwaffe pilot. He says Manchester United have been lucky. I tell him: 'They will probably go on and win it.' It is a throwaway remark. I never considered that they would. Not for a moment.

I had gone back to Luton by the time they played in the fourth round at Hereford. When the draw was made, the presenter had made a joke about this being a possible shock: 'You never know, Manchester United might win.' That's how the club was regarded then.

However, in that month in Manchester I had got myself back to fitness. I had trained hard, and because I was living in a hotel, I could control what I ate. After training I would go back to the hotel and watch television all afternoon and then go for a walk. The club sorted me out with a car. By the end of the month's loan, I had lost a stone and four pounds.

Mark Crossley arrived from Nottingham Forest as cover for Leighton and remained as United's reserve keeper until April, when he was recalled by Brian Clough. By then, Ray Harford had been sacked by Luton. Jim Ryan, who had played for the club in the 1970s and been Harford's deputy, was promoted to take over. Under him, Luton would win their last three games and survive on the final day of the season.

I felt I was on the verge of getting back into Luton's first team when Ryan rang me at home.

'Do you fancy going back to Manchester United for another month?'

'Do squirrels squeak?'

By now, Manchester United have beaten Hereford, Newcastle and Sheffield United to reach the semi-final of the FA Cup. They will play Oldham at Maine Road.

Oldham are in the Second Division, but they are a very good side who have just reached the League Cup final, where they will play Nottingham Forest. They are much, much better than United over the ninety minutes, but the game finishes in a 3–3 draw. Alex Ferguson feels that Jim Leighton is at fault for two of the Oldham goals.

Ferguson had known and worked with Jim for a long time. They had won two league titles together at Aberdeen. Jim had been part of the side that beat Bayern Munich and Real Madrid to win the Cup Winners' Cup. When he managed Scotland, Ferguson had taken Jim to the World

Cup in Mexico. However, the longer Manchester United remain in the bottom half of the table, the more the crowd turn on Jim. He can hear voices behind his goal in the Stretford End telling him to 'fuck off back to Scotland'. The stress eats into him. He develops migraines and ulcers. He wants Ferguson to say something, to back him publicly in a press conference. The supportive words don't come, perhaps because Ferguson doesn't believe he has the backing of United's fans any more, perhaps because deep down he knows the Stretford End want him to fuck off back to Scotland as well.

Jim needs help, but there's nobody at United to give it to him. That's what happens in football. When you struggle, you get no sympathy. You are alone.

Before the replay, Ferguson sees Archie Knox and tells him he wants to drop Jim. 'Don't,' says Knox. 'It will destroy him.'

Jim is in goal for the replay at Maine Road. In the first few minutes of the game comes the kind of incident that makes you think Manchester United are going to win the FA Cup. A shot by an Oldham player strikes the bar and cannons down. Everyone on the United bench thinks it has gone over the line. If the referee had awarded a goal, they would not have complained. The referee plays on. Oldham hit the frame of Jim's goal three times, but United win, 2–1. Just as he had at Nottingham Forest in the third round, Mark Robins scores the winner.

On the Saturday, I make my debut for United, not because Ferguson has dropped Jim, but because he has strained his kicking leg in the replay. We are playing Queens Park Rangers. We are sixteenth, two places above the relegation zone.

There is no question of ticking off the games as we wait for the FA Cup final to come around. It's all too important. United win 2–1 at Loftus Road. It is a tremendous result that gives the club breathing space. As the game is in London, Ferguson says I can stay down there and report back on Tuesday morning. That evening, United will be playing at home against Aston Villa, who are challenging Liverpool for the title. Jim Leighton will probably be fit, so the QPR match would in all likelihood be my only game for United. Before I leave the dressing room, I turn to the rest of the team and say: 'Thanks a lot, lads, that has made my season.'

When I arrive at the Cliff on Tuesday morning, it is to face the thunder in Ferguson's voice. 'Where the fucking hell have you been? We've been trying to fucking ring you. You're playing tonight.'

I had spent the weekend in London, eating like Billy pig. Non-stop lasagne and pork pies, all washed down with about three million cups of tea. I feel out of condition and very taken aback that I'll be making my home debut for Manchester United at such short notice. Ferguson tells me to do a warm-up and then get back to the Ramada and have a kip. What follows will rank as one of the best three games I have ever played.

Aston Villa are having the kind of season that will get Graham Taylor the England job once the World Cup in Italy is done. They go for us. I save a David Platt shot from two yards out while I am on the floor. It strikes me on the arm and flies wide of the goal. A close-range header from Tony Cascarino hits me on the knee. I must have made a dozen saves.

In front of me are Steve Bruce and Gary Pallister, known to everyone in the dressing room as Daisy and Dolly. Despite the names, they're the kind of defenders who give you confidence, who will look out for you. United win 2-0, a result that pushes the club up to fourteenth, ten points clear of the relegation places.

I am in the dressing room at Old Trafford, lying in the bath with Alex Ferguson, and the first thing that comes into my mind is that I can use this result to get myself a better club car. United's commercial manager, Danny McGregor, had given me a Volkswagen Jetta. The car is absolute crap. I know I am there for only a month, but who do they think I am? The fucking kit boy? I ask the manager if he could sort me out with something a little better, the kind of car the rest of the team are driving. At that precise moment, McGregor puts his head around the door to ask if some of the players could go upstairs to do some presentations in the sponsors' lounges. From the bath, Ferguson points at me and says: 'Get him a decent car, Danny. Tomorrow.' I am given a Volvo 760 GLE Turbo. It is dark blue, with leather seats, air conditioning, electric everything. Did I tell you I've always liked nice cars? I think I'm well in with the manager.

Stars in Their Eyes

There was no communication from the club. As far as West Ham were concerned, Joe Sealey had suffered a career-ending injury, his contract was void and his insurance would be settled by the Professional Footballers' Association. Technically, he was no longer their concern. His wages were paid for August and September, and then they stopped. Their final payment to him had been £4. In the days after Les's death, Luděk Mikloško had phoned. 'Do you want to come into training? I know you can't play in goal, but you could kick a ball at a few of the keepers. Chat with the lads. They would love to see you.'

Joe mumbled a refusal. He didn't want to mix with anyone. He didn't want to reply to questions that went: 'I'm so sorry, mate. Is there anything I can do?'

Not unless you can raise the dead.

West Ham did send the club doctor to visit Joe at home. Joe liked him, he seemed decent enough. He arrived in a suit and tie.

'How are you?'

'I don't feel right.'

'I know. The shoulder has been dislocated and torn three times, and you're still only nineteen. You might have to accept it will never be right.'

'No, it's not my shoulder, it's my head. I don't feel right in the head.'

'A lot of people have issues when they finish with football. Especially at your age. Especially at nineteen.'

'It's not that. I feel like I killed my dad. Listen, he coached me since I was a boy. He'd seen the injury, he was having to sort out the insurance, he was worried about what I was going to do. I'm qualified for nothing. If he hadn't had all that stress on top of him, he might not have had the heart attack. Do you see what I mean? I feel responsible for his death.'

Joe knew what the response would probably be: 'Your father died of catastrophic artery failure. Stress would have played no part whatsoever in his death.' Instead, the doctor looked at him, paused and said: 'I can't tell you that's not true.'

For years afterwards, Joe would roll that phrase around in his head.

George carried on playing at the West Ham Academy.

Before each game he would stare in the mirror and tell himself: 'Play well. Make him proud, push on for the old man.' He did play well. He did perform. However, for George Sealey to have made it at a Premier League club, there would have to be a rash of good seasons, he would have to avoid serious injury and his mental focus would have to be fiercely strong. Youth-team coaches have a dread of sixteen-year-old footballers who discover life has greater horizons than a training pitch, shuttle runs and repetitive practice.

Like his father and brother, George suffered from shoulder injuries. Gradually, as his body started breaking down, his motivation drained away. There was insufficient metal in his soul. He left West Ham for Crystal Palace and when he realised he would not make it as a professional footballer as his father had done, there was a sense of relief rather than grief. He started playing semi-professionally for Thurrock, where the Dartford Bridge reaches the Essex shore of the Thames. One day, he walked into his mother's bedroom and said: 'I can't do this anymore.' That was football done.

The day after Les's funeral, Jonathan Barnett offered Joe a job as an agent, working at Stellar's offices in a large Edwardian house near Marble Arch. 'Look,' Barnett said, 'you're eighteen, you know young footballers, why don't you look after them for us?'

Barnett's constituency was football club chairmen. They

had been used to dealing with agents like Eric Hall, who had grown up in Bethnal Green, made his name publicising T. Rex and the Sex Pistols, was seldom without an outlandish cigar and thought everything was 'monster, monster'. Barnett seemed the essence of reserved respectability, a prominent member of St John's Wood Synagogue who knew his way around a wine list. His family had owned casinos, but he had the knack of making a football director feel like they were not taking a gamble, that they were not obviously about to be ripped off.

However, the journey that led to Barnett exchanging anecdotes in the boardroom had not been a comfortable one. In the late 1980s, the London Stock Exchange had been deregulated – the Big Bang. It was a time of men in red braces holding brick-sized mobile phones and flicking through Filofaxes while making reckless promises. Roger Levitt was what Del Boy Trotter might have been, had he moved from Peckham to the Square Mile. His East End patter provided him with his nickname: 'Roger Rabbit'. His Bentley was chauffeur-driven, his cigars imported from Cuba. Champagne was his drink of choice. He dealt in pension funds. Boxing too: Lennox Lewis was his major interest.

In 1989, Levitt's business collapsed, with debts of £34 million. Barnett lost a serious sum of money; so, too, did Sebastian Coe, singer-turned-actor Adam Faith and author Frederick Forsyth.

Barnett was still fascinated by sport, and football in particular. He had met Lawrence Lustig through boxing and asked the photographer if he knew anyone who might be able to give him an introduction to the game. Lawrence suggested Les Sealey: 'He's coming to the end of his career. He knows everyone and he won't talk to journalists.'

They met at Barnett's house, near Lord's cricket ground. Barnett was already managing Brian Lara, who in the spring of 1994 had broken the world record for the highest scores in both first-class and Test cricket. At the kitchen table, they planned how they would take on football. It would be more lucrative than selling cars. It might be a lot more fun than rusting away on the Fylde coast with Blackpool.

The agency's first piece of business did not quite create the same headlines as those lauding a phenomenon who was touted as the greatest batsman the game had seen since Don Bradman. It was the transfer of Leslie Jesse Sealey from Blackpool to West Ham United. No fee was payable. By the summer of 2001, Stellar was the biggest football agency in the country. It would soon become the biggest in the world. Barnett may have felt he owed Les's son something.

His partner was David Manasseh. He was younger, brasher. His uncle owned the Café de Paris club, off Leicester Square, where Noël Coward and Marlene Dietrich had once headlined the cabaret. Manasseh would have been entirely at home back in the age when Coward was singing a risqué version of 'Let's Do It', before Dietrich, dressed in top hat and tails, crooned 'One for My Baby'. He had gone to Harrow and might have played cricket for Somerset had he not chosen to go into property. He did play for the MCC and lived in Lancaster Gate. In the 1950s, he would have been one of the fast set, switching effortlessly between the City of London and country-house parties in an open-topped Jaguar. In 2001, his job was to find footballers. Barnett would sort out the contracts.

Joe did not feel especially comfortable sat next to Manasseh as he tore down the motorways of England, not in an open-topped Jag but in a Porsche Carrera, a phone fixed permanently to his ear.

'You need to go to games,' Manasseh had told him in between phone calls. 'You need to sniff them out. You need to find people of your age – eighteen, nineteen, twenty. Don't watch the first-team games, because they're full of people who have made it. Go to the reserves, look out for people who haven't made any headlines.'

When he was alive, his father had told Joe the key to being an agent: 'Don't bullshit, don't over-promise. Don't tell a young lad you'll get him a move to Liverpool or Manchester United. Just say that however far he goes in his career, we will look after him.'

It seemed a simple ask, but Joe found it difficult to motivate himself even to get dressed. The process of getting to Marble Arch was even harder. Stellar had presented him with a black BMW to replace the Fiesta, but he knew only one way of driving into central London. That involved getting on the M25 north until it reached Barnet, and then following the Edgware Road all the way south until it reached Swiss Cottage. He was habitually late. When he made it to his desk, he found he had nothing to say. The telephone stared back at him, imploring him, taunting him to pick it up. He usually resisted. When his phone did ring, he didn't answer.

He could not face going to games because he would be watching footballers who still had a future, a future that had been denied to him. He would pretend he had been, and when Stellar asked for a recommendation, Joe would look up the match report on the internet and name someone who had been mentioned two or three times.

When he received Joe's suggestions, Manasseh would ask: 'Did you get their phone number?' Then Joe would *have* to go, to places like Stevenage or Boreham Wood, which hired out their grounds to Arsenal and Tottenham for reserve team games. He would wait, with an increasing sense of dread, in the players' car park for the target to arrive. He knew now how the *Daily Mirror* trainee must have felt, knocking on the family's door after Les's death. When the footballer arrived, Joe would stammer, mumbling something about how well he'd played. Sometimes there would be a brief exchange about West Ham or Les. Sometimes it might go well. Sometimes Joe would start the ignition on the BMW and realise he hadn't asked for the player's number.

He didn't want to be in Marble Arch. He wanted to be in Chadwell Heath, at full stretch in the mud, his gloves wrapped around a ball. And if he couldn't be there, he'd rather be in bed, blotting it all out. Asleep. Because when you're asleep, you're just like everybody else. He had no interest in finding young footballers and propelling them to stardom, because he himself was a young footballer and he had been propelled nowhere except to a place he did not understand. He wanted Glen Johnson to succeed, but the rest of them could join him in failure.

It wasn't long before the footballers he had left behind did just that. The West Ham side that went into the 2002/3 season – David James, Glen Johnson, Michael Carrick, Jermain Defoe, Paolo Di Canio – stood comparison with any in the club's history. Bobby Moore's boys had won the FA Cup in 1964 and, a year on, the Cup Winners' Cup. A decade later, Mervyn Day, Billy Bonds, Frank Lampard Sr and Trevor Brooking reached the final of the Cup Winners' Cup, before going on to win another FA Cup in 1980. This year's model, however, got themselves relegated. Joe revelled in their fall. He wondered how the Lampards would have reacted. Or Harry Redknapp. At best, their feelings would have been mixed.

Sometimes, lying in his room, Joe would make calculations. At West Ham, he had been one of the best half-dozen keepers in his age group. Goalkeepers were a close-knit group. They all compared themselves to each other, seized on each other's gossip and wondered who would be the first to break through. In Chingford, he had lived next door to Martin Brennan. They had been at Chase Lane Primary, in the same year as David Beckham's sister, Joanne. Brennan had got himself a move to Charlton, who had just been promoted to the Premier League.

Chris Kirkland was ahead of everybody. Like Joe, his father had taken a central role in his development, training him obsessively. While Les was a professional goalkeeper who had appeared in five major cup finals, Eddie Kirkland operated cranes, sometimes on twelve-hour shifts. He still found time to drill Chris relentlessly. When he was fifteen, Eddie bet £100 that his son would play for England. The odds were 100/1. Chris would regard the bet as a noose around his neck. By the time he was eighteen, he had already made his first-team debut for Coventry. At twenty, he was transferred to Liverpool for £6 million, at that point the highest fee paid for an English goalkeeper. The national manager, Sven-Göran Eriksson, was calling him 'the future of English goalkeeping'. However, Chris was betrayed too often by his own body to ever claim the future. There were too many injuries, although his father's bet earned him £10,000 when Chris played for England against Greece at Old Trafford.

Then there was Lee Grant, who had been part of Watford's youth teams but had now travelled up the M1 to

Derby. In 2002, he would make his first-team debut. There would be an England Under-21 cap, a career with Sheffield Wednesday and eventually a move to Manchester United, although not in the way Grant would have imagined in his bedroom back in Hemel Hempstead: at the age of thirty-five, he agreed to become United's third-choice keeper, an understudy to an understudy. At £30,000 a week.

Stephen Bywater was Joe's direct rival for a place at West Ham. Joe suspected that his dad had wanted Stephen to succeed almost as much as his own son. Les had given Stephen lifts to Chadwell Heath, which is something he had never done for Joe. He was a mentor, fiercely protective of Stephen's talents.

Stephen had been almost as riven by Les's death as Joe. When he heard the news from Southend, he asked Glenn Roeder if he could change his shirt number to 43, which had been Les's age at his death. From then onwards, Stephen thought Les was still watching over him. If he was in need of advice or caught up in a moment on the pitch, he would think to himself: 'What would Les do?'

Only Martin Brennan failed to make it. He played one league game for Cambridge before disappearing into the hidden vastness of the non-league game. Sometimes Joe thought he might phone Stephen or Martin, but, really, what was the point? What would he say? He no longer even watched football.

The Cup Final

I'm at the post-match party for the 1990 FA Cup final at the Royal Lancaster Hotel, opposite Hyde Park. It's a strange affair because nobody has won the FA Cup. The final between Crystal Palace and Manchester United finished in a 3–3 draw.

As the drinks are poured and the players stand around in little clumps, the mood among the men from United is one of relief. We were awful at Wembley, played off the park by Palace.

I went over to watch the game with the throng of photographers, sitting alongside Lawrence Lustig behind the advertising hoardings, well placed to observe the chaos that overwhelmed both defences. But for two goals from Mark Hughes, one of them coolly taken late in extra time, and Bryan Robson's performance, this would have been a wake. There's a sense of gratitude that we have a replay on Thursday. Defensively, we cannot be any worse.

I glance at Jim Leighton. He looks like he has gone through torment. He didn't play particularly well, but the waves of Palace attacks had stretched United's defence to the limit. There had been no easy way out.

He'd been stressed coming into the final. United had been beaten 2–1 at Tottenham, and Jim had played very well. However, the last away game of the season had been at Nottingham Forest, and we were thrashed, 4–0. For twenty minutes at the City Ground, the game had gone totally out of control.

I will always vividly remember walking into the dressing room at Wembley after the game and seeing Jim in the corner with his head in his hands. Anyone who has ever played under pressure like that knows how wiped out you feel by the end of it. The stakes were much higher for United than for Palace. Palace had beaten Liverpool 4–3 in the semi-final. Earlier in the season, Liverpool had thrashed them 9–0 in the league. Palace were up for it. This was their first final.

We needed to win. United had finished thirteenth this year, as we had the year before. When you see the television highlights of the game, the camera focuses in on Bobby Charlton, who is Alex Ferguson's biggest supporter in the corridors of Old Trafford. John Motson talks of 'turbulence in the boardroom'. Ferguson's had his four years.

He knows it. So does the chairman, Martin Edwards. So do the players.

Jim reckons Ferguson has lost the dressing room. I don't know, I haven't been here long enough. Perhaps there are some on the fringes wondering what it might be like with another manager. Bryan Robson? Nah. Steve Bruce and Gary Pallister? Has he lost Daisy and Dolly? Mark Hughes is an interesting man. He is very quiet, but he has played at Barcelona and Bayern Munich and has insights that none of the others do, insights that make you think. He knows how big clubs work.

Anyway, I am going to get another drink when Ferguson comes over to me.

'Do you know your loan period is up?'

'Yeah, I did know. I'm sorry I'll miss the replay.'

'Do you want to be involved?'

'Definitely. If the club wants me to be involved, I'll help in any way I can.'

'Don't worry, you'll be fucking involved.' Then he walks away.

Not long after, Ken Merrett, the United secretary, comes across and says I will have to be re-registered for another week. I had been planning to stay in London after the final as I thought my involvement with the club had ended. Ken tells me that I need to go to Luton on Monday to be re-registered. I am granted another four days as a Manchester United player.

I phone Alex Ferguson from Kenilworth Road. 'When do you need me back?' If there wasn't much for me to do, they would probably want me in on Wednesday morning, when they would be travelling down to the team hotel.

'I need you straight away.'

I drive to Chingford, fling some stuff together and make my way up the motorway to Manchester. By Monday night, I'm back in the Ramada.

I drive to the Cliff in the morning. We train, and when the rest of the squad go over to play a five-a-side, Jim and I do some specialist goalkeeper training. It involves me giving Jim the kind of practice he wants – firing in crosses, giving him different types of shot to save, advising him on his ground work. Anything he thinks needs tightening up. I hadn't thought I'd be doing any work, but after ten minutes the manager walks up and says: 'Les, do some work. Do some crossing, do some punching, and do quite a bit of it.' He walks away.

This is the first time the thought crosses my mind that I might actually be playing in the replay. It is the first time it occurs to Jim that he might not be involved.

On Wednesday morning, we travel down to Burnham Beeches in Berkshire, the hotel we stayed at before the first final. It's the one the England team use before games at Wembley. They have portable goals that can be used on an area near the front of the hotel, which is where we train straight after lunch.

The building is a Georgian manor house. There is a terrace with white ironwork tables and chairs, where guests can take afternoon tea or watch the swans in the lake glide by. Businesses use the hotel for conferences. Burnham Beeches is the type of place where a husband might take his wife for a weekend break. Or somebody else's wife.

When we finish training, I'm one of the last to walk into the hotel. Ferguson and Archie Knox are sitting in those wrought-iron seats near the hotel entrance. Just as he had before the semi-final replay, Knox had stuck up for Jim. He'd argued that the lads wouldn't stand for it. Jim was much more popular than me in the dressing room. I wasn't liked. Too brash, too London.

Ferguson had reminded Knox of something Jock Stein once told him: that he wouldn't go out for dinner with half of the players who had won him trophies at Celtic. The two men had weighed up our attributes. Jim was braver, I was a better organiser, but as Ferguson summed it up: 'Les Sealey is not a better goalkeeper than Jim Leighton, but he thinks he is. Right now, that's what matters.'

As I walk up the steps to the hotel entrance, the manager calls me over.

'I am playing you tomorrow.'

'That's fine. Have you told Jim?'

'No, don't you worry about that. Leave that to me.'

I say something about doing my best for him and for Manchester United. Then I go into the hotel.

I am in shock. I have played a grand total of two games in the entire season. I've hardly kicked a ball in anger. I think it's an astounding decision, and a brave one by Ferguson. If United lose, that decision alone will be enough to hang him. His job is on the line, not to mention my reputation.

I go to my room, which I'm sharing with Russell Beardsmore. When I enter, he's sat on the toilet with the door open. I say: 'Guess who's playing tomorrow?' Russell bounds out of the loo and says: 'Fucking hell.' His trousers are still around his ankles.

When I walk into the big, wood-panelled room that has been set aside for the team meeting, I sense straight away that everyone knows. Nobody looks at me, nobody smiles, nobody makes a little joke. The atmosphere is cold and sullen. Gary Pallister comes in late, goes over to Steve Bruce and asks what was going on. When Steve tells him, he looks shocked. Gary and Jim share the driving when they go to training. Now he's got someone behind him he barely knows. Gary's also got a dodgy ankle. He's already thinking tomorrow might be a long evening.

Jim is not at the meeting and he doesn't join us for the evening meal. He is rooming with Brian McClair. I go upstairs and knock on his door. Jim is alone, sitting on the edge of his bed in tears. The decision has utterly destroyed him.

If you have ever played football at any level, from Sunday mornings to the Premier League, you will know what it feels like to be dropped. It affects your pride, your state of mind, your confidence in yourself as a player and a person. Jim was trying to cope with being dropped for a cup final. He was destroyed.

I mumble something about Jim having my medal once the game is over. He says: 'I don't want your medal.' He adds that he doesn't blame me and that he wishes me well for tomorrow night: 'Go out and win the cup.'

Tomorrow night comes all too quickly. I am now the one under enormous pressure. If United lose, any chance of another game with them – let alone a contract – has gone. While I'm getting changed, the manager comes and sits beside me in the place nearest the dressing-room door. He asks me how I'm feeling, whether I'm all right.

'Don't worry, gaffer,' I smile at him. 'You've already won it.'

I'm being very blasé about it. At least, I am in front of Alex Ferguson. My arsehole is going sixpence, shilling, half-crown, manhole cover.

People often ask if you enjoy the big games. I can sympathise with any professional footballer who says no. Who wants to take the walk from the dressing room to the centre circle, hoping you are not the one who makes the mistake? Who wants to be the man that costs his team the cup? Who wants to make the glaring error in a 1–0 defeat?

In 1983, United played Brighton in the FA Cup final. The match was drawn, 2–2. United won the replay 4–0. If you ask the average football fan what they remember about that final, it will be the moment on the Saturday afternoon when Gordon Smith blew a chance to win the cup for Brighton in the last minute. Michael Robinson sends him through. The commentator shouts: 'And Smith must score,' and from five yards he hits it straight at Gary Bailey. Smith was never the same after that. He went to Manchester City and then had a brief spell at Glasgow Rangers before he faded from the big time, playing in Austria and Switzerland. Each move took him further away from Brighton.

How often does he replay the incident? Once a day? Once a week? Does the scuffed shot catch him unawares when he's in the shower or out driving? If he ever went back to the Goldstone Ground, it would have hit him full in the face: the Brighton fanzine is called *And Smith Must Score*. All schoolboys instinctively understand the dream of winning the cup. The fear of losing it is something that is never mentioned in the playground.

Anyway, I can't delay things any longer. The teams have been told to line up. It's time to face the music and dance.

We are standing in the tunnel at Wembley. All the Crystal Palace players seem to be looking at me. They are glaring. They seem to know I am the weak link. 'Christ, you're an ugly bastard,' says one voice. 'Less of the bastard,' I say. When somebody else makes a comment, I just tell them to fuck off.

As we go out, Jim is making his way to his seat. He is

being pointed at, mocked as he sits down. I am amazed he has turned up to watch us. I know many, many footballers who would have taken the first train home.

In the fourth minute, Mark Bright clatters into me and gets himself booked. Then Andy Gray flattens me. There's a change to Palace's tactics. On Saturday, everyone praised Steve Coppell for the way his team attacked, for their fluid football. Tonight, they are much more physical, much more ready to mix it. Every time I go for the ball, there is some contact.

I am not quite the lame duck they think I am. Firstly, I am motivated. Of course, I have been thinking about what might go wrong, but I have also been thinking about what might happen if Manchester United win the FA Cup with me in the team. It might not lead to world stardom, but it will lead to something. Also, I am the fittest I have ever been. I had trained very hard during my month back at the Cliff, and my fighting weight at Wembley is twelve stone ten pounds, instead of the usual thirteen and a half stone.

In the first half, Palace have a free kick, which they take an age over. I am shouting at the wall that I can't see the ball. Gray's shot comes straight through it, and I save with my legs.

Palace fade away. They put too much into the first game, and when Lee Martin scores after making a thirty-yard run from left-back, they have nothing left to give. I kick the ball upfield, and the whistle goes for full-time. Manchester

United have won the FA Cup, and so has a bloke who has spent most of his season with Luton reserves.

After getting my medal, I see David Pleat, who is now manager of Leicester. I am a bit full of myself.

'You never rated me, did you?' I tell him.

'Oh yes,' he says. 'I've always rated you.'

When we get back into the dressing room, Jim is sitting in the same corner as he did on Saturday. This time he's wearing the club blazer and tie. I offer him my winner's medal. He says no. I go over to Bobby Charlton and ask him if he could give it to Jim. 'You shouldn't do that,' he replies. I ask if he could do it anyway.

In the Crystal Palace dressing room, there are a lot of exhausted tears. Mark Bright is throwing his loser's medal against the wall. Somebody picks it up, puts it back in its box and tells him to keep it. When he shows it to his gran, she smiles at him and tells him: 'Well, you can't win them all.'

The baths at Wembley are huge, waist-high when you stand in them. Alex Ferguson is next to me in the bath. He suddenly seems younger. We chat about the match, and I ask if I can stay in London, go home to the family. He says yes, and adds that he'll give me a call in a few days' time. I imagine he'll offer me a few grand as a thank you, but I can't imagine there will be a contract. It may be a long time before I see him again. I certainly won't be sharing another bath with the manager of Manchester United.

When I leave the dressing room in my blazer, Lawrence is waiting. 'Get the cup and I'll take a photo of you.'

I don't want to – I'd rather just get home. With Wembley now still and empty, he tells me to lean against one of the goalposts, holding the FA Cup.

'You might not want this now,' he tells me. 'But in years to come you'll be glad you had this picture taken.'

My Night with Mrs Thatcher

The traffic jam is endless, bright lights everywhere as we edge on to the North Circular, deep into a lovely spring night. There are flags flying, scarves everywhere, people on car roofs. There's a soft-top motor crawling alongside us, four or five inside, one sitting on the boot. The chaos is absolute. This is the first time it really hits me how much this game has meant to Manchester United.

I am being driven by Lawrence, who has offered me a lift back to Chingford, where we both live, in his 1.6-litre Ford Sierra. As we walked across the Wembley car park, he had said to me: 'You know what you've just done?'

'Well, we've just won the cup. What point are you trying to make?'

'You realise they have to give you a contract? You have just saved that man's job.'

'Actually, one of the directors did come over and said they'd look after me. In the dressing room after the presentation. It might be cash rather than a contract, and even then I don't know. You know how it is. Things are said and then they're forgotten.'

I put my kit bag in the back of the Sierra. I'd been told I could keep the kit as a souvenir.

As the traffic chugs on towards the turn-off for the M1, the United fans edging towards the left-hand lane, which will take them north, there's a car right next to us. I wind down the window and look at the driver.

'Where have you all been? What's been happening tonight?' I ask, wearing my Manchester United blazer, although the driver can't see the badge.

'United have just won the FA Cup, you daft bastard.' He looks at me as if I have just come from Jupiter.

'Who did they play?'

'They played Crystal Palace. They won 1–0.'

'Didn't United change their goalkeeper or something?'

'Yeah, they put Les Sealey in goal instead of Jim Leighton, and he didn't half play fucking well.'

I'd been unzipping my kit bag as I was talking to the lad, and now I hold up my goalkeeper's jersey.

'Do you think Les Sealey had one of these?'

He looks at the badge and looks at me. There is a split

second as his face changes from puzzlement to recognition. 'It's fucking well you, isn't it?'

By now, the traffic has come to a complete standstill. People are actually getting out of their cars and talking. Then the bloke shouts to no one and everyone: 'Over here! It's Les Sealey!'

We explain we need to be in the lane over to the right. People begin shouting: 'Let them through, let them through. It's Les Sealey.' A Red Sea of cars parts, and we swing away to the east.

As we disappeared, a few of those left behind might have asked each other why I wasn't on the team bus or in a hotel drinking champagne. Others might have wondered what a Manchester United player was doing in a Ford Sierra.

The *Sun* had called Elaine even before the final whistle had sounded at Wembley. Their first offer had been a thousand pounds. Elaine told them she doubted very much whether I would agree to be interviewed. Fifteen minutes later, they rang again. The journalist told Elaine that he had 'had a word with his editor' and they could offer £5,000 if I would talk only to them.

By the time I reached the door, the offer had gone up to twenty grand. Elaine handed me the phone. I listened for a bit, said: 'No, thank you,' and put the phone down. I was sure the price of the interview would have been to talk about how Jim Leighton had come to be dropped. I wasn't going to drag another goalkeeper down – I couldn't do it to Jim, not even for £20,000. I sat down to celebrate with a cup of tea, a couple of ham sandwiches and a large Havana cigar.

Despite not actually speaking to anyone, I was still all over the papers. There were 'twenty facts you didn't know about Les Sealey'. Did you know Les was in the Boy Scouts? Did you know Les is a practical joker? Did you know Les used to own a Jensen Interceptor? It was all done from cuttings. It was everything you could possibly want to know about Les Sealey, except his reaction to winning the FA Cup and what he thought of Jim Leighton.

I kept the kids off school on the Friday and took the boys to a toy shop. I left my mum to answer the phone. When anybody rang, she claimed to be my housekeeper and told the reporters that I'd gone out for the day.

While I was out, a photographer from the *Daily Mail* knocked on the door and asked my wife if I would have a photo taken with the family. Elaine said: 'Please don't be here when he comes back. Do yourself a favour and go away.' The photographer said he understood, but he had to ask the question and wouldn't bother us again.

As I walked up to the toy shop, a guy in a Jaguar XJS stopped his car, allowed the traffic to pile up behind him and clapped me all the way to the entrance while he stood in the middle of the road.

Meanwhile, life became hell for the Leightons. They were trapped in their home in Wilmslow and had to call the police to clear the press from the front garden. What made the stress worse was that Jim's season was not over. He was due to go to the World Cup in Italy. Up until the FA Cup final, he had been Scotland's first-choice goalkeeper. Now, he wondered where he stood. In less than a month, Scotland would be playing their opening game against Costa Rica. Would he be dropped by his country, just as he had been dropped by his club?

In the end, he wasn't. Scotland stayed loyal. Jim played in all three of their games and told me that going to the World Cup – which was his third with Scotland – was the best thing that could have happened because he was able to blot out the memories of Wembley. If Brazil hadn't scored a late goal in Turin, Scotland would have qualified for the knockout stages.

However, when he came back, he was finished at Manchester United. The FA had sent the club Jim's winner's medal, but when Ken Merrett handed it over, Jim wouldn't accept it. Alex Ferguson called Jim into his office and told him he should accept the medal because it would be something he would want to show his grandchildren. Jim told the manager there was nothing about the 1990 FA Cup final that he wanted a memento of. United didn't even give him the dignity of an immediate transfer. During eighteen months of purgatory, he trained with the reserves, had a couple of loan spells at Arsenal and Reading and played one game for United – a League Cup tie at Halifax, who were then bottom of the Fourth Division. United held out, finally allowing Jim to leave after receiving an offer of £150,000 from Dundee.

The FA Cup was United's first trophy in five years. There would be a parade through the city, starting at Old Trafford and finishing in front of the Town Hall in Albert Square. There would be a civic reception, a banquet and a party – all the things I absolutely cannot stand. Anyway, I was busy. I'd promised to go to Wanstead cricket club's annual quiz with Lawrence, my bank manager, Steve Miell, and our wives.

The parade was on the television in the bar. I was asked why I wasn't in Manchester. I smiled and said Wanstead had asked first, and it would have been rude to have stood them up.

When I sat down at the table, I said to the rest of the team: 'Even if I wanted to go, I don't think I'm entitled to be there. My contract ended on the final whistle on Thursday night. I'm not actually a Manchester United player any more.'

By the way, we won the quiz. The prize was a bottle of wine.

On the Tuesday, I got a call from Alex Ferguson. He would be at Heathrow in a couple of days and wanted me to meet him in a hotel near the airport.

I went to his suite, where he offered me a cup of coffee and handed me my medal. Bobby Charlton had given it to

'You might not want this now. But in years to come you'll be glad you had this picture taken.' Les on the pitch with the FA Cup, 17 May 1990.

After Luton reached two Wembley finals in 1988, Les posed to show how at home he felt at the old stadium. He was being overconfident. Luton were thrashed by Reading in the Simod Cup final and he missed the League Cup final through injury.

Les in the photographer Lawrence Lustig's garden where he was hiding to escape the press the day after the 1990 FA Cup final.

'I wanted to be a pro just for one year, just to see what it was like. After that, they could let me go. I'd work as a mechanic.' Coventry kept him but Les never lost his love of cars.

The Sealeys at home in Chingford. From left to right: George, Elaine, Les and Joe.

Joe and George pose with an equally young Kasper Schmeichel and Alex Bruce at Old Trafford.

'We are all actors: goalkeepers. We all pretend to be people we are not.'

The glittering prizes: Les at home with his Cup-Winners' Cup and his FA Cup winner's medals.

With the Lampards, the Redknapps and the Sealeys, West Ham's training ground resembled a small family business. Shaka Hislop stands between Les and Joe.

'The United fans chant "Always Look on the Bright Side of Life" and break into choruses of the James song "Sit Down". Sit down is all I can do – I can barely stand.'

him. He then offered me a contract for the 1990/1 season. The basic wage would be £1,250 a week. When he offered me a signing-on fee of £70,000, I nearly fell off my seat. I don't think for a moment I would have been offered a contract if Crystal Palace had won the FA Cup.

Ferguson said the club would help me find a house. Very soon I would be living in Wilmslow with the rest of them. Luton were only too glad to get my wages off their books and paid me £17,500 to settle my contract. If you include the bonus for winning the FA Cup, those three games for Manchester United had earned me nearly a hundred grand.

When the story got out that I had tried to give my FA Cup medal to Jim Leighton, I was nominated for a *Daily Star* Gold Award. The ceremony would be at The Savoy Hotel in London, and I would be presented with my award by the Prime Minister, Margaret Thatcher. Joining me at The Savoy were people who had performed outstanding acts of heroism. Someone who had saved a family from drowning when trapped in their car in the River Ouse. Or someone who had dragged people from a burning building. Or a bomb disposal expert. Then there was me.

At the start of the ceremony, they showed a film of those to whom the awards were being given, explaining why they were receiving them. You had the same stirring feeling as when watching *Gordon of Khartoum* or *Custer's Last Stand*. Then the audience was shown a film of Les Sealey playing football. It was, to say the least, embarrassing.

When Mrs Thatcher handed me my award, she had been prime minister for eleven years and had won three general elections. After meeting Les Sealey, she lasted a couple of months before she was gone.

I'm not one for awards, and I'm not really one for medals. What am I going to do with my FA Cup winner's medal? I could keep it in the house and get it out and look at it if I'm feeling low or nostalgic, although I suspect it won't be long before our house is broken into. It'll probably end up in the bank, where I will never see it. Realistically, I should send it to Christie's and ask them to sell it, and then sit back and read headlines about my 'greed' and 'lack of respect' for the competition and for Manchester United. A medal creates an awful lot of problems.

What I do think about is that in fifty years' time there will be a history of United published, and I will be in it. There will be a chapter devoted to the 1990 FA Cup final, and my name will be mentioned. It will be there in the text: 'Sealey'.

In 1992, Alex Ferguson published a book called *Six Years at United*. After the final, he said that it was 'animal instinct' that made him drop Jim Leighton, a recognition that it was a question of survival. Now, he was saying that if he had his time over again, he would do things differently: he would keep Jim in the side. I happen to think that if he had his time over again, Ferguson would do exactly the same thing, because fundamentally he is a ruthless man.

You can say what you like when you've won. What if Montgomery had not won the Battle of El Alamein? He wouldn't have become Field Marshal Montgomery, Viscount of Alamein. He'd have been packed off to a home for retired generals. There, he would have spent his time banging on about how impossible it was to fight a genius like Rommel and why the Matilda tank was the biggest piece of junk ever assembled. You can be generous when you've won.

Careless People

One by one, Joe Sealey's friends were purged. Not deliberately, not consciously, but they were erased from his life.

There were other places to go, other people to seek out. He would go to Charlie Chan's, a nightclub built beneath Walthamstow dog track. There would be Tottenham players there who had migrated from the more sedate surrounds of Epping Forest Country Club. They would be joined by members of the *EastEnders* cast. Leslie Grantham would hold court, and then, as Phil Mitchell replaced Dirty Den as the focus of the soap opera, so would Steve McFadden. Always mingling, gliding through the crowd like sharks through a shoal of sea bream, would be the men who imagined themselves as the Ronnie and Reggie of the new millennium. The club and track were owned by Philip Chandler, the cousin of Victor Chandler, who had made millions in online gambling. One day, Philip would be found dead in the swimming pool of his villa on Mexico's Pacific coast. His son did not believe it was an accident.

At Charlie Chan's or Faces, another footballers' nightclub in Gants Hill, Joe was outgoing, sociable in a way he seldom was back home. He got talking to a good-looking man with dark, swept-back hair, whose tanned face carried with it a hint of Botox. His name was Michael Edwards-Hammond. Joe had first met him when he was working for Stellar: first, in the offices of a London tax firm, where he was introduced to him as a 'film and television consultant'; and then at The Ivy, where Stellar would entertain their clients.

Joe could talk, and he had stories about training with West Ham and growing up with a father who had won trophies with Manchester United. Edwards-Hammond had better ones. He could talk about dating Dannii Minogue or sharing a girlfriend with Prince Andrew. He was in films.

He had grown up the son of a painter and decorator in Bexhill-on-Sea, a town that suffocated in its own gentility. It was known chiefly for the De La Warr Pavilion, an art deco theatre on the seafront that opened in 1935 – 'just in time to be bombed', said Spike Milligan, who was stationed in Bexhill during the war.

Edwards-Hammond would do or say almost anything to avoid having to return to Bexhill, and if it meant changing his name or inventing some family history, then so be it. The truth was unlikely to come out. Unless her career went drastically wrong, Dannii Minogue would not be appearing at the De La Warr Pavilion.

Edwards-Hammond was talking to Joe at Charlie Chan's. He pointed to the ceiling, in full flow.

'You know, David Beckham used to work upstairs at the dog track. Collecting glasses for a few quid.'

'I went to school with his sister,' said Joe, voice raised over the music. 'I met him in a record shop in Wilmslow, actually. We had a really good chat. Lovely guy.'

It would have been 1996. He had introduced himself, as he always did, as 'Les Sealey's son'. They had talked for nearly half an hour about football and music. Beckham was on the cusp of an extraordinary journey. He had just met Victoria and had broken into Manchester United's first team. He was astonishingly good-looking. He was also completely unaffected, relaxed, polite.

It was a good story, good enough to impress Edwards-Hammond. If Joe knew people like David Beckham, he might be worth having around. 'I know Wilmslow. I can introduce you to some of the *Coronation Street* mob,' he told Joe. 'You'd like them. They're more fun than the *EastEnders* crowd who come here. Come round mine on Friday. I've got an apartment in Canary Wharf, I'll drive you up.'

The streets where Edwards-Hammond lived seemed more Isle of Dogs than Canary Wharf, but at least there was a Range Rover parked outside the two-bedroom flat. At Keele services, he asked Joe if he fancied driving it the rest of the way to Cheshire. He was twenty years old, skimming along in the fast lane of the M6 at the wheel of a Range Rover, sat next to this man who seemed to know everyone.

The Rectory did not seem the obvious gateway to drug addiction. It was a Georgian-fronted pub in Wilmslow that sold Timothy Taylor's Landlord and offered Cajun salmon and chicken in mushroom sauce.

There was someone in there from *Coronation Street*. Someone famous. They talked about Wilmslow, the capital of the Cheshire footballers' belt. Joe knew it quite well. Les had lived there when he played for Manchester United.

Les had been impressed by how relatively modest Alex Ferguson's house had been for someone who managed the biggest football club on Earth. His pride and joy had been the snooker room, where the table stood on a vivid tartan carpet.

Joe was told the Fergusons no longer lived at Fairfields. They had moved somewhere bigger, somewhere more in keeping with where the manager of Manchester United might be expected to live. Apparently, it had turrets.

They left the Rectory with a group of people, some of whom Joe had not been introduced to. They clambered into the Range Rover and headed past the airport and into the heart of Manchester. The actor had an apartment near Deansgate. They were talking about *Coronation Street* and the news that after three decades as Mike Baldwin, Johnny

Briggs was leaving Weatherfield for the golf courses of Florida. 'For his final scene he needs to go on the roof of the Rovers with a machine gun and start mowing everybody down,' said Edwards-Hammond. 'Like Jimmy Cagney in *White Heat*. "Made it, Bet! Top of the world!"'

From the window, Joe looked down on the traffic sliding past far below. Most of the activity was in the kitchen. There on the side, by the cooker, was a small pile of white powder. He was nudged. 'Go on, son. You don't know till you've tried.' Joe went over to it. He had never even seen cocaine before. Should you put some on the tip of your tongue to test its authenticity? Should you chop it up with a credit card? He fumbled for something suitable in his jacket. Eventually, he rolled up a ten-pound note and inhaled. Suppose they were trying to trick him? Suppose it was washing powder, Daz or Omo? He'd say: 'Yeah, that's pure Colombian. From Medellín rather than Cali, if I'm not mistaken.' And they'd all be falling back on to the sofas pissing themselves.

It was instant. Immediate. It was quicker than vodka. A feeling that he was a good person washed over the front of his brain. It made him happy, and he couldn't remember the last time he had been truly happy. He wondered why he had never done it before. More than that, he realised that, twenty years old or not, he belonged here among this crowd. These were his people. Back in Loughton, those he had known all his life, his family, no longer seemed to have anything worth saying.

There were more trips to Manchester. More encounters with the people from *Coronation Street*. More drugs. They would meet in the Victoria and Albert Hotel, across the way from the Granada Studios. The rooms took as their theme Granada's television hits. There was a *Coronation Street* suite with china ducks flying up the walls. The room dedicated to *The Jewel in the Crown* was done up like a maharaja's boudoir. One fuzzy, hungover morning, Tony Wilson, who ran the Haçienda nightclub, woke up in the V&A to be confronted by a large photograph of himself presenting *Granada Reports*.

The actor was not one for bullshit. He had worked hard to get his part on *Coronation Street*. It had begun as a small role, but he had developed it. The part had grown bigger, and there was something inside him that knew it might be the biggest he would ever play. Those around him were different. F. Scott Fitzgerald had described the entourage around Jay Gatsby as 'careless people', careless in every sense of the word. To Joe, those in the room were brilliant, glittering personalities with nothing weighing on their shoulders.

One was Raymond Nevitt, whom the *Manchester Evening News* would describe as a 'flamboyant fraudster'. He lived in Bowdon, where house prices would be recognisable to anyone who lived in the Surrey countryside. Some nights Joe would stay there.

To Nevitt, speed meant fast cars rather than drugs. In

2001, he had taken his white Ferrari into the Gumball
Rally, where owners of other expensive cars raced from Pall
Mall to St Petersburg and back on public roads. It was an
attempt to recreate the spirit of *Monte Carlo or Bust!* but
instead of Tony Curtis and Terry-Thomas, there was Damon
Hill in a Lamborghini and the comedian Vic Reeves in a
Mercedes-AMG.

Nevitt wrote the Ferrari off in Latvia. The wreck was
taken back to be the centrepiece of a champagne reception,
paid for with someone else's money. Nevitt had borrowed
£3.5 million on forged documents. His house was no longer
available to Joe because Nevitt was on the run. After four
years he was arrested in Cape Town and spent nine months
awaiting extradition in Pollsmoor Prison which had once
housed Nelson Mandela.

To Joe, the Victoria and Albert's main attraction was
the people and the fact that some of them had access to
cocaine. He had not yet steeled himself to buy any; he had
not yet learned to identify a drug dealer by the way they
moved, the way they made eye contact. There would come
a time when he could spot a dealer the moment he walked
into a pub.

He met his first in Faces in Gants Hill, and from then
on, Manchester began to lose its pull. Joe had never really
liked nightclubs, but now there was a reason to go.

In the summer of 2002, nearly a year after Les's death,
Michael Edwards-Hammond asked Joe if he wanted to go to

a movie. It wasn't James Bond, it wasn't *Lord of the Rings*, but it was a premiere.

As they drove towards Leicester Square to watch *Scooby-Doo*, Edwards-Hammond became increasingly irritated as the traffic congealed around them. When he realised there was nowhere on Tottenham Court Road to park, he leaped out of the Range Rover, pointed at a driver who had just manoeuvred into the last available bay and screamed: 'I'm CID, move your fucking car.' The man did exactly that, and Edwards-Hammond negotiated the Range Rover into the now-empty space. He grinned at Joe. 'If you say it like you believe it, people will do anything you tell them to do.'

Afterwards, they found themselves going down the steps into what was then London's coolest nightclub. Chinawhite was on Air Street, just off Piccadilly Circus. In the words of the *London Evening Standard*: 'The music is awful, the drinks prices exorbitant and the entry process humiliating.' However, if your pockets were deep and your face fitted, you might catch a glimpse of George Clooney or Liza Minnelli on the dark teak dancefloor. However, when Alex Ferguson was presented with a photograph of his goalkeeper, Fabien Barthez, coming out onto Air Street at gone three in the morning, he fined him £40,000. Even by the standards of Chinawhite, it had been an expensive evening.

Much of Chinawhite was lit by candles. As you passed the bar, you went into a small room, divided into booths, that was reserved purely for the A-list. As Joe got used to the light, he glanced into one of the booths, to be greeted by the sight of Chris Eubank dressed as Fred from *Scooby-Doo*: blue shirt, white sweater, orange neckerchief. The boxer's then-wife, Karron, had come as Daphne.

Joe had only come for the cocaine. He could not fathom the amount of money needed to buy a drink or the bullshit that was being talked in the booths. He wanted just one thing, and when he found it, he was glad to go. Like his father, social events would become things he wanted to leave.

The Knee

I am lying on the pitch at Wembley looking down at my knee. There is a four- or five-inch cut that goes right down to the bone. When the flap opens up, I can actually see the inner workings of my knee.

It is the 1991 League Cup final between Manchester United and Sheffield Wednesday. We are playing as badly as we have done all season, and now Paul Williams has just run through on goal, to be closed down by Steve Bruce and Gary Pallister. He has got off a shot that went wide, but the pitch is wet and he has slid into me. There was no malice in the challenge. It was an accident.

There is no pain at first. I don't feel the skin rip on his studs. It is only when the referee, Ray Lewis, who is a few feet from me, looks down that I feel there might be a problem. There is a look of fear and almost disgust on his face. He yells at the Manchester United bench.

Bryan Robson is the first United player to come over, and he crouches down, puts his hand on my shoulder and tells me to stay where I am. He is joined by the United physio, Jim McGregor. He takes one look and says: 'Forget it, you'll have to come off.'

But I still don't feel any pain. Perhaps my body is in shock, perhaps it's been flooded with adrenaline, but I think I can cope. There's no blood coming from the wound. I shout: 'Jim, I'm going to stand up. Let's see how it is.' Bryan and Steve say they will help me off the pitch. I completely lose my rag. I can see the stadium clock: there are twelve minutes left. The only replacement on the bench is Mal Donaghy. Someone will have to go in goal, and we are 1–0 behind. I can make it through the last dozen minutes.

Bryan tells Jim to strap the knee up. It bloody hurts when I take a goal kick, but Daisy and Dolly protect me so well that I don't actually have a shot to save. The problem is that apart from one header from Brian McClair that he tips over the bar four minutes from time, you could say the same of Chris Turner in the Sheffield Wednesday goal. The final whistle goes while I've got the ball in my hands, and soon the Wednesday manager, Ron Atkinson, is on the touchline giving interviews. He'd invited the comedian Stan Boardman on to the bus to give the players a pep talk during the journey from the team hotel to Wembley. He won't be able to shut him up on the way back to Yorkshire.

It's when I start climbing the steps to collect my loser's

medal that the pain begins to kick in, because by now all the adrenaline of playing has drained away. Coming down, I lead with my injured knee, and now the pain is starting to take my breath away.

I don't join the team when they go over to thank the Manchester United fans. Norman Davies, the kit man, helps me to the dressing room. There, I'm put on the table in the middle and the club doctor puts five stitches into the wound. There's no anaesthetic. 'Be careful, doc,' I say as the first stitch goes in.

'Les, you've done your job. Now just let me do mine.'

I have a shower and change into the club blazer, but it is while we are on the coach going to Heathrow that the knee becomes tighter and tighter. I can feel it swelling with every mile. Jim comes down the bus, takes a look at the knee and tells me to go straight to hospital. He adds: 'I know I'm just the physio, not a doctor, but if it were me, I wouldn't get on that flight.'

Elaine had come to Wembley to watch me play. The year before, I'd asked if she wanted to see me play in the FA Cup final replay, but she told me that she didn't want me getting stressed about having to sort out a ticket. I should just concentrate on my goalkeeping.

This time, she is with me in the departure lounge at Heathrow, where we are told the flight to Manchester has been delayed. I am on crutches, trying to walk off the pain, but it gets worse and worse. Elaine tells me I look ashen and clammy. By the time the flight is called, I can't stand any more. I simply lie down on the floor, which is cool, black linoleum, and let the sweat from my face drip down on to it while somebody phones for an ambulance. I hear a shout of 'Twenty minutes'. Nobody from Manchester United stays with me, they all board the flight. Elaine remains in the now-deserted departure lounge, holding my hand. The pain is by now indescribable. By the time the paramedics are giving me gas and air, I am in tears of agony.

It is when we arrive at the hospital very late in the evening that I encounter some luck. As I am being wheeled in on a trolley, a surgeon is leaving for home, dressed in a blue anorak. He turns round and walks back in alongside me. He tells them to take me to a cubicle and remove my trousers. He takes one look at the knee and says: 'Take him to the operating theatre. I'll phone around and get some people in.'

By midnight, they are prepping me for the operation. I tell Elaine to book herself into a hotel and I'll see her in the morning.

'You'll be all right,' the anaesthetist says as she puts a mask over my mouth.

'I am sure I will be.'

When I come round, the surgeon is still there, standing over the side of my bed. My eyes focus on the clock, which says two thirty. He leans over and whispers: 'Who's a lucky boy then?'

My mouth is too dry to make words, my brain too groggy to think of any.

When I wake again at seven in the morning, the surgeon says that I had been stitched up at Wembley with dirt and grass inside the wound. It had taken a litre and a half of saline solution to clean the knee out. There had been pus in the joint, and I was getting blood poisoning.

'Let me tell you what would have happened if you had got on that plane,' he says. 'It would have delayed the operation by four to five hours. The flight to Manchester's only about forty-five minutes, but you would have arrived at close to midnight. Whatever hospital you went to would have had to assemble an operating team and prep you for it. At the very least, you would have had full-blown blood poisoning, and that's you laying on your back for the next few months with a drip in your arm. What's more likely is that the pressurised cabin would have intensified everything surrounding the wound and your leg would have had to be amputated. Worst case, we would have been burying you.'

Even now, even in these circumstances, my mind flits to the final of the Cup Winners' Cup, which is in twenty-two days' time. I have no chance of playing in the second leg of the semi-final against Legia Warsaw at Old Trafford, but we had won the first game 3–1 in Poland and were pretty confident of going through to face either Barcelona or Juventus. I ask the surgeon what my chances of making the final in Rotterdam are. He replies: 'Absolutely none. You are lucky to have two legs.'

Elaine comes to see me the next day, still wearing the cup final suit she had bought for the occasion: a red jacket with a black skirt, layered with beads. As she comes through the ward, the other patients must think they are being visited by the Duchess of Kent.

I am kept in hospital for eight days. When I get back to Manchester, Jim McGregor the club physiotherapist, after telling me I could sue the club for negligence, works on my knee every day to reduce the swelling. I tell him I can't threaten Manchester United with lawyers. It would end my career, and there is still part of me that wants to play in a European final, however unlikely it might seem.

The obvious decision would be to bring Jim Leighton back for the second leg of the semi. He was Scotland's World Cup goalkeeper; he has the experience to go straight back in. However, he and Alex Ferguson are still not speaking to each other, and that overshadows everything. Ferguson chooses Gary Walsh. He is a youth-team player, a talent who in 1987 becomes Manchester United's first-choice keeper. Gary must have looked at his future and seen it stretched out in front of him.

Then there's a little jolly to Bermuda, which everyone on that plane must have relished. However, in a nothing friendly, Gary is kicked in the head and is so badly concussed that Ferguson brings in his old friend, Jim Leighton, from Aberdeen. Gary returns to the shadows of reserve-team football. That's how it goes for goalkeepers.

Gary starts his comeback pretty well. Legia Warsaw can only manage a 1–1 draw at Old Trafford, which sends us through to meet Barcelona in the final. He then keeps a clean sheet as United win the Manchester derby. What does for him are the two games before the final, both of which are in London. First at Highbury against Arsenal, who had cruised to the title, and then against Crystal Palace. United concede three in each game, and Gary does not play well at Selhurst Park.

That makes up Ferguson's mind. He tells me it is psychologically important that I play. I have my first training session at the Cliff on the Monday after the Palace game. The final is on the Wednesday. I spend about twenty minutes dealing with crosses. I can't dive, can't run. There are still stitches in the knee. We are playing Barcelona. They are the first really big team we've met in the competition. Our first two ties saw us travel to a mining town in Hungary to play in a stadium that held 7,000. Then we faced Wrexham, who had won the Welsh Cup. We beat them 3–0 at Old Trafford, and then had a European away trip that involved taking the coach down the M56. By half-time we were leading by two goals, 5–0 up on aggregate. We would be at Derby on Saturday, so we just eased through the gears. It was a perfect evening.

Aston Villa had been given a rather more taxing assignment in the UEFA Cup. They were defending a two-goal lead at Inter

Milan. As I came off after the Wrexham game, a steward told me that Inter had won 3–0. I was last into the little dressing room at the Racecourse Ground, and as I pushed open the door I said: 'You won't believe this, lads – Villa are out.'

Ferguson looked at me: 'Fucking sit down, you.' Then he addressed the cramped room. 'If you think I'm accepting that, then you've got another bloody thing coming. You coasted that, and let me tell you, no Manchester United side of mine coasts a game of football. Ever.'

Montpellier are a big step up. The first leg is at Old Trafford in March. It's streaming down with rain and most of the pitch looks like washed mud. Brian McClair scores after a minute, which should have calmed everyone down, but then a low, rather aimless cross comes in. The only people in the penalty are me and Lee Martin, who is standing on the six-yard line. Lee promptly side-foots it into his own goal. I just stand there.

The manager says nothing to Lee at the interval, but by the finish the match has become frenetic. Three minutes after half-time, Mark Hughes appeared to have been punched by their defender, Pascal Baills. Baills was sent off, but the French don't think he touched Hughes. Not only do Montpellier hold on with ten men, they almost snatch the game in the last minute. Their captain, Laurent Blanc, thinks we have cheated, and Ferguson is asked by the French journalists about 'English fair play', as if this were 1935 and we were playing lawn tennis.

When he finally comes into the dressing room, the manager is in a murderous mood. His eyes catch Lee. 'Do you want to stay in football?' It's not a question that invites an answer. Sensibly, Lee lets the manager continue. 'You've got a wife to support, you've got a baby to look after. Well, you won't be fucking supporting them at Manchester United.' He gets nearer and his voice becomes slower and more menacing. 'You do something like that again, son, and you'll be out of the bloody game.'

I've heard a lot of dressing-room bollockings in my time. I've been the target of quite a few. But this was horrible, and we all knew it was gratuitous. The manager was simply overwhelmed by the frustration of the evening and was looking for a victim. Lee was twenty-three, a local lad from east Manchester. I don't think he was ever the same again. His touch, his confidence, his instinct seemed to desert him. I don't know if it was because he had scored an inexplicable own goal in a European quarter-final or because every time he closed his eyes he saw his manager's face pressed against his own.

Ferguson made his mind up about Lee that night. He didn't play in the return leg in France. Clayton Blackmore, who replaced Lee at right-back, scored, which might tell you about how sharp the manager's instinct can be.

Lee isn't in the squad for the final in Rotterdam. Over the two seasons that follow, he plays just one league game for Manchester United. He is as finished at Old Trafford as if the manager had walked into that dressing room and torn the red shirt off his back. In 1993, he will be sold to Celtic. When he returns for Mark Hughes' testimonial and runs into Ferguson in a corridor at Old Trafford, the manager just looks straight through him.

Lee Martin was the man whose goal in the FA Cup final had saved Ferguson's career. Gratitude can only stretch so far. At this level and at this club, footballers are like battery hens. As long as we keep laying the eggs, our cages are heated and lit and the food keeps coming. As soon as we stop producing, they cut our heads off.

When we fly to Holland, Ferguson decides to take an extra physio with him, an old Scottish guy called Jimmy Steel who used to train boxers and spent years with Celtic. He isn't afraid to launch into a Scottish folk song as he massages my knee as we prepare to keep Johan Cruyff's dream team at bay.

This is United's first European final since they won the European Cup in 1968. Sir Matt Busby is in the stands of the De Kuip Stadium in Rotterdam, and so are about 50,000 others from Manchester. There are flares being set off in the open stands, where there are also plenty of umbrellas. It is pissing down. My knee is strapped and bandaged.

Early in the game, I run to make a clearance, and Julio Salinas, Barcelona's big centre-forward, beats me to the ball by about four yards. The ball is funnelled away from danger, but it is an interception I would normally have made with ease. You'd better be careful, Leslie my boy, otherwise you're going to make a complete fuck-up of this game.

Because I haven't trained properly for several weeks, my muscles have wasted away, and as time wears on, my left knee, which is encased in bandages, stiffens up. It hurts when I kick the ball, and several times I struggle to get across my goal.

At half-time, with the scores level, Ferguson tells me my kicking has been shit. I reply that it's windy down at pitch level. He turns round and says: 'Don't make any fucking excuses.' As we go back out after the interval, I think to myself that if United lose this final, I will be vilified for playing. I cannot expect any protection from the manager.

Barcelona are without their regular goalkeeper, Andoni Zubizarreta, and Carles Busquets is making his debut in the final. He makes a right hash of our first goal, beaten by a header from Steve Bruce that Mark Hughes toe-pokes over the line. Then Hughes, who endured a terrible time at Barcelona, scores as good a cup goal as you'll see, taking the ball past Busquets and driving it into the net.

Then comes the first real shot I've had to face in the final. It's a free kick from Ronald Koeman that flies through the wall. Had I been fully fit, I reckon I would have saved it with my nose, but I just cannot make the ground up and it goes in.

There are eleven minutes left. Eleven minutes of chaos. Barcelona have a goal disallowed for offside. I punch one ball clear and it bobbles around the area before Clayton Blackmore hacks it away. Steve Bruce sells me short with a back-pass. I haven't the speed to make it but I manage to scramble it away, and when the ball comes back in, Michael Laudrup's shot is cleared off the line by Clayton.

Every time we ask the referee how long is left he seems to say: 'Five minutes.' I can see Gary Walsh warming up on the touchline, and if the game goes into extra time, I know I am coming off.

Then the whistle goes, and I lie flat on my back, the rain falling on to my face. I don't feel elation, just sheer relief that it is all over. When I reach the dressing room, the only person who asks how I am is a Manchester United director, Amer Al Midani. He tells me I look awful and wonders whether I need a doctor. I say I'll be okay. Another director surveys the scene in the dressing room, where champagne is being sprayed everywhere, and says: 'It's not as if they've won the league title, is it?' It is Manchester United's first European trophy in twenty-three years. I feel like punching him.

I now have to go to the medical room because I have been selected for a drugs test. By now I have removed the bandages from around my knee and walk in wearing just a T-shirt and shorts. My leg is completely bald from the top of my shin to halfway up my knee. All you can see are the stitches. Salinas and Koeman are in the room. Salinas looks at my leg and shakes his head, while Koeman says: 'I don't know how you played with that.' He informs me that Barcelona thought I had fully recovered from the injury. I am amazed Cruyff hadn't been told how vulnerable I might be. They ought to have been looking to pepper me with shots.

As I wait to wee, I start thinking about all the medication, all the painkillers I've taken, because there will be an awful lot of stuff in my urine. Are any of them banned? I hope Jim McGregor has done his research, otherwise I'm fucked. The test is clear.

I can't go up for the presentation because I can barely walk. I sit on the bandstand while Bryan Robson lifts the cup. Nobby Stiles collects me and takes me back down to the dressing room, while the United fans chant 'Always Look on the Bright Side of Life' and break into choruses of the James song 'Sit Down'. Sit down is all I can do – I can barely stand.

Birthday Boy

'Ah cocaine, such an amusing drug, don't you think?' Princess Margaret once said to Mick Jagger. It had made Joe Sealey more than what he once was. He had always carried a sense of humour, but now he was screamingly funny. He had always been talkative, always had an opinion, but now the words flew out. He was not famous as his dad had been, the shoulder had seen to that, but he now hung around with people who had that glitter.

However, after a while cocaine began to possess him. It no longer wanted him to go out and share himself with anyone else. It wanted him to itself. It wanted to be alone with him. Theirs was the only relationship that mattered. The only relationship there was.

It was Joe's twenty-first birthday, 12 March 2004. His nan had invited him round for a Chinese takeaway. He left quite quickly and drove to a BP petrol station in Debden and bought a bottle of Jack Daniel's. He had with him seven grams of cocaine. He was living in a converted manor house in Chigwell, which had been divided up into flats. Once he shut the doors, he never wanted to leave. There was a farmhouse with a country pub nearby. It was almost rural. It was a good place to live if you did not want to be disturbed, and Joe did not want to be disturbed. Ever. He started by getting rid of his girlfriend, who had become an inconvenience. It meant cutting ties with her sister's boyfriend, who was a drug dealer. That was more of an inconvenience.

He was an addict now. Duller, slower. It seemed not to matter. He no longer saw the point of going out, wasting money talking to people when all he wanted to do was be alone with it. He would listen to the phone ring and then fall silent. He had no interest in who was calling – they could not possibly offer more than what he had here in this room.

He didn't notice the downfall of Michael Edwards-Hammond. The Range Rover had been exchanged for a Mercedes worth £105,000, although, naturally, he had not paid for it. The celebrity photographs had become more exotic. There was one with Elton John, another taken with the Princes William and Harry when he turned up for a polo match at Windsor. Sky Sports were so impressed they allowed him to front their admittedly sporadic polo coverage.

Edwards-Hammond had promised his girlfriend a private tour of Windsor Castle. They were waved through the Henry VIII Gate, the entrance used by members of the royal family. They spent an hour in Windsor's private gardens before a policeman asked them what they were doing. Edwards-Hammond was arrested and charged with being a public nuisance. Another eleven counts of impersonating a police officer and wasting police time were added in. At Isleworth Crown Court, he was described not as a film director or theatre producer but as a con man.

Joe's days drifted by in a fog of daytime television and long, remorseless nights. At one point, he realised he had been awake for three days. Cocaine takes away the need for anything except itself. It opens the arteries so more of it can stream into the body. Slowly it wrecks the metabolism, weakens the resistance.

In those three days Joe had not eaten. He realised he was starving. Pizzas, Chinese food and chips were ordered in, and the whole process began again. Even the drugs were home-delivered. He would barely move from the sofa and found himself weighing not fourteen but twenty-two stone. He was unconsciously begging for a heart attack. To go as his father had done.

Faith

I've just gone out to the shops. I think I might treat myself to a packet of Slim Panatellas. It's summer 1991.

While I'm out, the phone rings, and my mother, who is staying with us, picks it up. The voice on the other end says: 'It's Ron Atkinson. Is Les there?'

'He's gone for a run, Ron.'

'How far does he normally run?'

My mother, who can think on her feet, says: 'About three miles.' It's a good job she doesn't say 'six', otherwise Ron would have known that was a total lie.

'What's Les doing next season, Mrs Sealey?'

'Well, I think he's coming to play for you now, Ron.'

My mum goes out to look for me and tells me Ron Atkinson has been on the phone. When he rings back, I tell him I'm doing nothing next season.

After the Cup Winners' Cup final, I had been to the Cliff to see Alex Ferguson about a contract for the 1991/2 season. I asked for the same terms as the previous season – £1,250 a week, plus a £70,000 signing-on fee.

'I don't think you'll get that. I don't think the chairman would give you that,' Ferguson said. 'You might get fifty grand.'

I was pissed off because what I was asking for was not a lot to a club like Manchester United, but it would be a lot to me. We had just won a European trophy. They then told me they were not prepared to pay any signing-on fee, just the £1,250 a week, which I could have got anywhere. They had taken stock and decided I was no longer so important to them. I knew the club was ready to sign Peter Schmeichel, and I knew he would be first choice.

The reason I knew United were going to sign Schmeichel was because I had recommended it. The club had sent me to Copenhagen to report on him. They'd been watching him since before the FA Cup final. He was twenty-seven, a Danish international who'd played at Wembley just before the 1990 World Cup.

Ferguson had already met him, but I don't think he was certain. Denmark is like Holland: it's quite easy to stand out in their league. Schmeichel did not just stand out, he seemed to have everything a goalkeeper required. It was obvious. I told the manager he should bring Schmeichel to Old Trafford. Having duly signed my own death warrant,

I asked if I could have a free transfer. The manager did not seem bothered in the slightest. What I did with what remained of my career was of no concern to him.

I contacted Martin Edwards to ask if I could keep the club car and whether we could do a deal on it. The book value of the Volvo was about £12,000, but given what I had done for United, the club would probably let me have it for quite a lot less. The chairman said: 'The car is the property of Manchester United, and if I let you have it for a discount, Les, I am technically taking unauthorised money out of the club. You can have the car, but it has to be for its full market value. I'm sure you understand.'

I thanked him, put the phone down and didn't understand. I wondered how a few thousand quid could matter so much to a club like Manchester United.

The next morning, the club phoned to say the manager wanted a word and would call later that day. My first thought was that a club had been in touch about taking me on, and I began to wonder which one it might be.

By half-nine that evening he still hadn't rung, so I phoned his home and spoke to his wife Cathy. 'Oh, Les, he's been trying to get hold of you. He says it's urgent. He'll phone tonight.'

Elaine started panicking. We began wondering what was so urgent that Alex Ferguson needed to phone us so late on a Tuesday night.

It was nearly quarter to eleven when the phone rang.

'Les?'

'All right, gaffer?'

'Listen, I need to talk to you. I don't think I looked after you when I said you could leave. It's been troubling me. Is there anything I can do?'

I told him about the Volvo.

'You should have come to me. You know the saying about the man who knows the price of everything and the value of nothing?'

'Oscar Wilde, gaffer.'

'Aye, Oscar Wilde. That's him, that's the chairman. Changes the fucking subject every time money comes up. I'll talk to him.'

I got the car. I drove it to Birmingham to see Ron Atkinson. Although he had won the League Cup with Sheffield Wednesday and got them back into the First Division, Ron had walked out of Hillsborough to join Aston Villa. The day after he phoned, I drove to their training ground at Bodymoor Heath. I was asked to join a five-a-side between the coaches and some of the players who had turned up early for pre-season. The full squad wasn't expected back until the following day.

Afterwards, I went to the canteen to talk things through with Big Ron.

'I've just sold my reserve goalkeeper, Lee Butler, to Barnsley for £250,000 and I need a good second keeper. I haven't been able to find anyone, so I'm asking you.' A big smile, then a pause. 'Well,' he said, 'what do you want?'

I didn't reply, I wanted Ron to show me his hand first.

'I can offer you £1,000 a week and a signing-on fee of £25,000.'

'Do I look like I come from fucking Hartlepool?'

Ron laughed and took a big gulp of tea. 'Don't fuck about, Sealey. What do you want?'

We settled on a thousand a week, plus all the win bonuses, which I would get whether or not I was playing, plus a signing-on fee of £35,000. It was slightly less than I would have got at Manchester United, but I would have more chance of first-team football at Aston Villa, have a longer contract and would still be playing for one of the biggest clubs in the country.

Ron's first-choice keeper was Nigel Spink, but he told me: 'I don't care about names. If you're good enough, you'll play.'

I was an Aston Villa player. Well done, Mum. There was, however, a problem. As I explained to Elaine when I told her what Villa had offered, I didn't think I would pass the medical. The problems with the knee had not cleared up during the summer. Whenever I walked, you could hear a clicking sound.

After speaking to Ron, I tried my knee out with a run around the park. I did a couple of hundred yards before I had to stop. It was agony. I had dived around a bit in the five-a-side at Bodymoor Heath, but I was wearing tracksuit bottoms and I knew my knee wasn't right.

When I got back from Birmingham, I told Elaine: 'I've agreed a contract, but as soon as I have a medical, I'm absolutely fucked. There is no way they are going to pay me to be a cripple. My career could be over.'

'In that case,' said Elaine, 'you will have to sue Manchester United.'

I had spent the summer trying all the specialists. I had had an MRI scan and seen a doctor at the London Hospital, an expert in sports injuries who was at a loss to explain why the swelling was still there.

I was at my wits' end, but I remembered that Bryan Robson had used a faith healer called Olga Stringfellow. He told me that he had been to see her with a hairline fracture of his shin bone. She had put her hands on his shin, and the next day when he went for an X-ray, the fracture had healed. Bryan absolutely swore by this story.

Desperate situations call for desperate measures. I was due at Villa on the Monday. I went to see Olga on the Sunday. Elaine and the boys drove down with me to her village in Hampshire. She was a lady in her seventies, living in a little terraced house. She had a faint New Zealand accent and told me she was in touch with a spirit who could see me in the room. He was an Indian gentleman. I thought she was absolutely scatty but decided I should just go through with it. I had driven this far, I couldn't just walk out now.

As I lay with my injured leg across her lap, she said: 'Sorry, love, I can only do this when I'm pissed.' She got out a bottle of vodka and poured herself a tumbler full. Elaine and I looked at each other, eyebrows raised as far as they would go.

The whole process took over two and a half hours. Her method of treating the injury was to put her hands on my knee. I felt a burning sensation, a red-hot iron scorching my skin. The sound of static electricity seemed to be coming from my knee. When we were back in the car, Elaine felt my knee through my jeans and it was still red-hot.

Olga said her spirit had told her there was also a problem with my ankle. This was a mystery to me – I had never had any trouble with my ankle. She took it, and I had the same burning sensation. She said the cost of the treatment would be £100 and that the injury would vanish in three days. The vodka in the bottle Olga had opened about two and a half hours earlier was already gone. I thought that this was wasted money, but then she looked at Joe, who would have been about ten. He was sitting on the floor, and Olga could see he had a bruise and scrape on the inside of his elbow where he had fallen over. She asked his name and whether he minded her touching his arm. When she did, Joe pulled away. 'Don't worry,' she said. 'It won't hurt you.' She touched the mark on Joe's arm, and he felt that same burning sensation.

The next day, when Elaine was taking Joe to school, she looked at his arm, and there was just a small red mark. The bruise and the graze had vanished.

I went to Bodymoor Heath on the Monday, but full training did not start until the Wednesday. I did it in my tracksuit bottoms, and I would sign a two-year contract with Aston Villa the following day. However, on the drive back home, the knee swelled up horribly. The first thing I said to Elaine was: 'I'm finished.'

I had a cup of tea and a couple of bacon rolls and went to bed. I must have slept for an hour. When I woke up, the knee was in perfect shape. The pain, the redness, the swelling had all gone. It was three days since I had visited Olga Stringfellow.

Damaged Goods

Slowly, day by day, Joe recovered. The feelings of disgust at what he had inflicted on his body began to seep through him as the drug had once done. First, he got off the sofa. Next, he left the living room, and then, blinking at the strange, bright light, opened the front door that led from the flat to the fields of the Essex countryside.

There were reasons other than the realisation that his body was on the edge of collapse that made Joe rebel against the constant infusion of cocaine and alcohol into his body. Dimly, he recognised he had to work. He needed to earn money. There is a cliff edge to addiction, when the price is not your job or your relationships but your home. Joe stopped before he careered into the void.

He went back to being a football agent. It was all he knew, and he felt a desperation to stay in the game. Cocaine did not let him go that easily. He would be on the road and there would be a hotel. The larger and more anonymous, the better. There would be less chance of a knock on the door and the call of 'housekeeping'. He became a functioning addict. That was a progress of sorts.

Football agents had increased their grip on the game. There were fewer obvious avenues, but Joe had the basis of a plan. The influx of foreign footballers into the Premier League had become a flood. On Boxing Day 1999, Chelsea had fielded a side that contained not a single Englishman. It was a portent for the new millennium.

The game itself was becoming unstable. Joe targeted young players for whom the route to the first team was no longer clear and older men desperate to stay in the game because to be outside it was now a frightening prospect. Perhaps because he was damaged himself, Joe found himself working with damaged people. He had a knack for understanding their needs.

The younger players could be persuaded to move down a division. He met Lee Sawyer, a midfielder who in September 2007 had been one of Chelsea's substitutes in a Champions League fixture against the Norwegian champions, Rosenborg. On the pitch were Petr Čech, John Terry, Joe Cole, Ashley Cole, Claude Makélélé, Michael Essien and Andriy Shevchenko; beside him was José Mourinho. The game was drawn, Mourinho was fired a few days later, and Sawyer, an eighteen-year-old from east London who had overcome a stress fracture of the back and a cruciate ligament injury just to get this far, would never play for Chelsea. He could, however, be persuaded to play for Southend and Woking.

Older players were more difficult. They not only needed to stay in the game but required money too. There were mortgages to pay, divorces to fund, addictions to feed. Joe told them they would not get what they wanted at Wrexham or Notts County, but they might if they were prepared to travel abroad. Across Europe and beyond, there was a demand for Premier League footballers. They would be offered a flat, a car and a considerable salary, perhaps tax-free. In short, they would be looked after.

In the summer of 2009, he persuaded Roy Carroll that he needed to be looked after in Denmark. Carroll was from Enniskillen and had played in goal for Manchester United, where his career had been defined by a single shot. It had come from the boot of Clarence Seedorf, in a Champions League fixture with AC Milan at Old Trafford. It was from distance and wasn't especially well struck, but it slipped from Carroll's gloves into the path of Hernán Crespo. It was the only goal of the game.

Like Jim Leighton remembering the FA Cup final, Carroll would close his eyes and see it. Always. He did not play for United for another two and a half months, before being brought back for the 2005 FA Cup final against Arsenal. It might have offered him the kind of improbable glory the 1990 final had handed Les Sealey. Carroll kept a clean sheet, but the match was lost on penalties.

He moved to West Ham. There was another FA Cup final, this time against Liverpool. He was dropped for it and his career disappeared into an alcoholic haze. By the time Carroll had completed a season with Derby that saw them finish the season with eleven points – the lowest total in the history of English top-flight football – he was separated from his family.

Carroll took Joe's suggestion and signed for Odense. Hans Christian Andersen was born there, and although the move was not quite a fairy tale – Odense finished second rather than first – Carroll was voted the league's best goalkeeper. He was intrigued by how many of his teammates cycled to training. He was given the space to breathe.

Some of the problems that faced Joe at Stellar were still with him. Unusually for an agent, he disliked answering his phone. Calls always meant trouble, and the worse the footballer he had offloaded, the more there would be. No player phoned to thank him for the flat he had sorted. No chief executive rang to emphasise how well the deal had gone. It was always something that needed fixing. By him.

He did not have the resources that were available to him at Stellar. Sometimes, if he wanted to send a message to a club in the Far East that he had a player available, he would type it in English, run it through Google Translate and send it. There might be enough of it that made sense for him to be invited to a restaurant in Chinatown, where he would be checked out by someone who said he was a friend of the owner in order to see if his knowledge of football was better than his command of Mandarin.

Once, the chief executive of a club in Thailand did call back. Joe sent him Alton Thelwell, who had been a defender for Tottenham and, after a series of knee injuries, was now plying his trade at Leyton Orient. The deal did not go through. If Thelwell's knee was ruined in London, it would also be ruined in Bangkok, but on the long flight back to Heathrow, Thelwell decided to confront the reality of his career and become a personal trainer.

Joe's life was changing. It was a Thursday night in late November, and he found himself in a nightclub in Epping Forest called 195. Rio Ferdinand and Ashley Cole had been on the guest list. The bar was busy. Joe had a trick when confronted with a queue for drinks: he would grab the attention of a woman in front of him and say, 'If you get me my drinks, I'll pay for yours.' It nearly always worked. This time, it didn't. The woman, who was older than Joe, looked him up and down and said: 'No.'

He asked her out. She refused but gave him her phone number. Eventually, they settled on Sunday lunch at the King William, a white, weatherboarded pub in Chigwell. Afterwards Joe agreed to put up a Christmas tree for Nicole. When he arrived at her home, there was no furniture, just a seventeen-inch television in the front room. He thought he had been duped, that Nicole was a squatter.

A Great Railway Journey

Once you walked through the leaded double doors everything about the Blind Beggar seemed dark. The floor, the bar, the wood panelling. There were metal bar stools, a few low tables and some leather banquettes. There were very few women – they had to be invited in.

On 9 March 1966, it was in the fiefdom of the Krays. Fort Vallance was half a mile away. That evening, George Cornell dropped in for a drink with a mate. He'd been visiting a fellow gang member who was being treated for gunshot wounds in Whitechapel Hospital.

A few months earlier, Cornell, who worked for the Krays' great rivals, the Richardsons, had met Ronnie in the very different surroundings of the Astor Club in

Mayfair. Although they insisted on black tie and entertained Princess Margaret, the morals of the Astor Club were not so very different from the Blind Beggar's. Prostitutes were served with the house champagne. The club paid the Krays £200 a month in protection money. George had marched up to Ronnie and called him a 'fat poof'. The audacity was breathtaking and so was his choice of boozer. It would take Ronnie, his driver, Jock Dickson, and his minder, Ian Barrie, five minutes. They would drive past some already-squalid 1950s flats, on to the Cambridge Heath Road and one right turn to reach the door of the Blind Beggar.

When Ronnie and Barrie march in, 'The Sun Ain't Gonna Shine Anymore' is on the record player. Cornell looks up from the bar and announces: 'Look what the dog has dragged in.'

Barrie fires into the ceiling. Ronnie fires his 9mm Mauser into Cornell's forehead. The record player jolts. All those in the shocked and silent pub can hear is Scott Walker singing 'any more, any more' over and over again.

After the Krays fell, the Blind Beggar passed into and then out of Bobby Moore's hands. By 1977, it is owned by the brewery, and little Nicole Hurley is upstairs being looked after by Jimmy, the manager, and his wife. Her mum, Ann, is downstairs behind the bar. The layout of the Blind Beggar is much the same, but they are trying to forget the Krays. The bullet hole made by the shot that killed Cornell is covered up by a picture.

In 1977, the Blind Beggar is no longer a place where money from organised crime can be laundered; nor is it a stop-off on Mad Frankie Fraser's tours of gangland, with day-trippers going inside to ask for 'a Luger and lime'; nor are there films about the Krays featuring Martin and Gary Kemp of Spandau Ballet or Tom Hardy. The Blind Beggar is trying to be just another pub. Women no longer have to ask permission to enter, and on Friday and Saturday nights, they and their men spill out on to the pavements, not knowing they are part of the last hurrah of the old, white East End, which has already changed and will continue to do so ever faster.

Along that part of Whitechapel Road, which locals call 'the Waste', the old markets still thrive, but the stallholders are now Bengali, descendants of the *lascars* who crewed the tea ships of the East India Company and who centuries later came to work in the cramped textile mills of Spitalfields.

Nicole's father was also an immigrant, but from Ireland rather than Bengal. Dermot Hurley was a policeman in Dublin and London, but before he met Ann he left the Met to become a car dealer. It says something for the way the police were regarded in the East End that Nicole was six months old before Dermot mentioned to his wife what he used to do for a living. The cars, now augmented by a scrap metal business, took him out of the East End and into the Essex stockbroker belt. He did not take Ann with him, and by the age of seven Nicole was spending half her time with her mother in an East End tower block and half with her father at a farmhouse where there were stables and where Rolls-Royces and Range Rovers competed for space on the drive, which was guarded by two stone lions. Her father could offer her showjumping at gymkhanas, a villa on the Costa Brava and a 65ft motor yacht moored in Gibraltar. If Nicole could close her eyes to his incessant womanising, it was an almost idyllic childhood. Or at least half of one.

Then came the recession of 1989, and Dermot was caught cold by the doubling of interest rates. He had invested heavily in a consignment of Kato hydraulic cranes, which were plodding their way through the Pacific swells en route from Japan when the crash came. They could neither be sold nor recalled and were travelling far too slowly to be of any use. Everything else – the Rolls-Royce, the Range Rover, the yacht – was on finance, so when Dermot Hurley went, he went quickly.

One day, Nicole came to the farmhouse, and not only had the cars gone, so had everything else inside. Even the radiators had been removed.

Nicole travelled. Her mother was from the Jewish East End, brought up around the beigel shops of Brick Lane. It was perhaps not a surprise that in order to escape the collapse of a girlhood paid for with borrowed money she ended up on a kibbutz by the Jordan River.

She returned to London on the Magic Bus that ran between Syntagma Square in Athens and Victoria coach station. There was nothing particularly magical about the bus, unless it was the ability of a twenty-year-old vehicle that did not have a toilet to keep going for five days continuously. To sustain her, Nicole had been armed with only a pack of biscuits and a bottle of water.

She went to Basildon, a new town that was created after the war as a workers' paradise, complete with bathrooms and indoor toilets for the bombed-out East Enders. It was far from Eden, but Nicole had inherited her mother's instincts for survival and her father's for sensing an opportunity. The railway lines that led west from Basildon swept past what was once West India Docks. The cranes no longer offloaded produce from the Caribbean, they were building the towers for the gleaming new financial centre at what was now Canary Wharf.

The Docklands Light Railway, until then a glorified train set that ran on eight miles of line, was being vastly expanded. There was no regulation of working hours and little of personnel. You could turn up and work as long as you liked. You could make as much as you wanted.

Nicole duly turned up at what was to become Mudchute station on the Isle of Dogs. The construction workers, mainly former British Rail employees, looked at her as if she had come in a ballgown. This had never been women's work.

A crane was lifting a lighting rig into position. Nicole looked up.

'You might want a second strap to hold that steady. It's going to come loose,' she shouted.

'Fuck off, Doris.'

The rig ripped free of its single support and crashed down on to the track.

The work was hard and relentless, and Nicole worked hard and relentlessly. One day, her supervisor asked if she knew anyone who wanted to work on the railway. Fridays, especially, were a problem. Rather than just give him names and phone numbers, Nicole formed her own little company, hiring out workers not just on the docks but at Luton Airport, where they were building a railway terminus. She ran it from her dining-room table and soon had thirty people working for her. When she came home, some would be asleep in the lounge waiting to head off for the night shift.

She now had a viable business, a husband and a daughter, Luca. High-heeled shoes had replaced the boots.

One day, Nicole was driving away from the beige towers of Harold Wood Hospital, which had already been ear-marked for closure. She had been told she had suffered a miscarriage. She had felt pregnant. There had been something inside her womb.

Then there would be more cramps, a gush of blood, another journey to the doomed hospital, where there would be a laparoscopy – a camera inserted into her abdomen – and someone telling her that she had miscarried once more.

At a roundabout, Nicole swung the blue pickup truck with its go-faster stripes 180 degrees, flung it into the hospital car park, almost ran into reception and shouted at the woman behind the counter: 'There is something wrong with me.'

By chance, a Dr Tebbit was in the reception area. She had written her dissertation on choriocarcinoma, or cancer of the uterus. There had not been a case of it at Harold Wood for fifty years, but she asked if Nicole would come with her for an immediate laparoscopy.

She was moved to a specialist unit at Charing Cross Hospital and operated upon that night. There would be six months of chemotherapy, of morphine, of her hair coming away in her hands. She came through it alive.

Nicole would have two more children, Kiera and Remi, but while her marriage survived cancer, it did not survive a young family. Ten months after the separation, Nicole decided to spend a Thursday night in a nightclub in Epping. She had made her way to the bar, was just about to order the drinks, when the big bloke behind her yelled that if she got him a Jack Daniel's and Coke, he would pay for her vodka, lime and lemonade.

It was a transaction that would save Joe Sealey's life.

In the Court
of King Ron

I am looking at Ron Atkinson, studying him. He's not the person people think he is. Ron comes over in the press as an international playboy, one who steps out of a white Rolls-Royce covered in jewellery and holding a glass of champagne. You'd probably expect him to time his training sessions with a diamond-studded watch.

Well, I am looking at his watch, and it's an ordinary watch. It looks quite cheap actually, and he's wearing no jewellery at all. I can't see any champagne anywhere in his office, though Ron does drink gallons of tea. He is far more into tactics, the nuts and bolts of football, than he lets on to the press. Big Ron is a bit of an act.

He treats me very well, although he often remarks that I

seem tired. He's right about that. When I joined Aston Villa, I decided I wouldn't move to Birmingham, commuting from Chingford instead. I'd get up at half-seven each morning, have breakfast, spend two hours on the motorway and then train. After lunch in the canteen, I'd drive home again, hoping to time it before traffic clogged the M1. I would then fall asleep on the settee for two hours. It's no way for a sportsman to live.

My heart and soul aren't really with Aston Villa. After Manchester United, everything seems like an anticlimax. Villa are a huge club with an excellent pedigree, but compared to United, there is something missing. As a United player you felt that everybody knew you, that everybody was watching you. It bred an attitude of us against the world, and the world we were ranged against was everybody who wasn't a member of our football team.

I don't get that sensation here. Villa are a big club with a big manager, but behind the scenes, they tend to think small. Sometimes, such as when they bought Dean Saunders, Villa will make a statement to show they can compete with the best, but I don't think Ron's ideas permeate the whole fabric of the club.

Villa's number-one keeper is Nigel Spink. He is a good goalkeeper, he is respected, he has won the European Cup, but I don't think Ron particularly rates him. I think he is catchable, and in October 1992, when Nigel falls ill, I have my chance.

We play Everton at Goodison Park and win 2–0. Villa win the next three. In four matches, I have conceded just one goal, and we are up to fourth in the table.

In the dressing room, Ron is different to Alex Ferguson. Before the second leg of Manchester United's League Cup semi-final against Leeds in 1991, Ferguson had come into the dressing room at Elland Road and said: 'Don't you dare lose, don't you dare fucking lose.' Lee Sharpe scored the winner in the last minute. Ron might go into the dressing room and announce: 'Come on then, entertain me.'

However, before long comes the game that seals my fate at Aston Villa.

It is January 1992, and we are at home to Sheffield Wednesday. Even before kick-off there is tension around the match. Ron's decision to walk out of Hillsborough to join Villa had caused an absolute furore in Yorkshire. When the fixtures came out, his first game as Villa manager was away at Sheffield Wednesday. He copped some dog's abuse on the touchline, which became worse when Villa came from two goals down to win 3–2.

Five months on, and it's the return game at Villa Park. Let's just say that, particularly in the home dugout and among the away supporters, there's quite a bit of emotion riding on the result.

With a few minutes remaining, a cross comes in from the right, and Nigel Jemson heads it downwards. It goes to my right, and I catch it six inches in front of my goal line.

However, my arms are in front of me and my body is over the line. I am actually lying over the ball. The linesman is on the other side of the pitch and he can't see the ball for my body. He signals a goal. All hell breaks loose.

The game calms down, but I don't. I spend the last minutes on the edge of my area, absolutely seething at the injustice. I cannot wait for the final whistle so I can tell the referee, George Courtney, and in particular the linesman what I think of them.

The whistle goes, and I sprint over to the officials, who have gathered in the centre circle. I shout at the linesman: 'You are a fucking cheat.' At that moment, the Sheffield Wednesday captain, Danny Wilson, comes across and drags me away. It is a good job he does, because by now I have totally lost control. Eventually, I am ushered away to the dressing room.

Five minutes later, a policeman comes to the door and tells me the referee wants a word in his room. Jim Barron, Villa's goalkeeping coach, goes with me.

When we enter, there are two policemen already there, as if they think I'm going to physically attack the officials. The linesman is sitting in a corner, staring at the floor. I feel nothing but contempt for him. If he were telling the truth, if he were confident of his decision, he would look at me. He does not have the bottle to admit he made a mistake. Courtney tells me I will be reported for bringing the game into disrepute.

After he says his piece, I run into Ron, who thinks I went way over the top. I tell him: 'I know there is nothing I can do about it, but the ball wasn't in the fucking net. It was not over the line.'

Ron goes over to handle the press, something he is very good at. He keeps them onside. Once he's in that press room, he's very shrewd. He tells the papers enough so they don't have to bother me for a quote.

What settles it for me when I watch the game on video is the reaction of our full-back, Dariusz Kubicki. He was the closest observer of the incident. Usually, if a defender thinks the ball is over the line, his reaction will give it away, stopping, grimacing or turning away for the restart. All Dariusz did was clap me and then move into position, ready for my kick upfield.

I am charged by the FA with bringing the game into disrepute, and despite all of Ron's best efforts to smooth things over, the media wants me hung from the highest tree. The *Sun* announces that Aston Villa should sack me and I should be banned from football *sine die*. The reason they are so hard on me is because I never speak to them. Everyone at Villa is expected to speak to the press, which offers them a kind of protection. I have been told that as a journalist it is quite hard to be critical of someone you speak to on a regular basis. It is quite uncomfortable to be at a training ground and then catch the eye of a footballer you have just butchered in print.

Just before I played my first game for Villa, at Everton, the guy from the *Sun* swaggered over like he owned the place and said: 'Can I have a word?' It wasn't: 'Do you mind if we talk about the Everton game for five minutes, Les?' It was expected, almost a contractual obligation. I said no, I didn't do press. So when the sky fell in against Sheffield Wednesday, I hadn't taken out that particular insurance policy. I was fair game.

When I am summoned to Ron's office at Bodymoor Heath, the papers are laid out on his desk. 'Look at these,' he says. 'They're a fucking joke.' Then he adds that I'm not going to be sacked and that he would have a go at the *Sun* at the press conference before Saturday's game at Manchester United. He does. He calls the paper 'a disgrace'.

He also fines me. He tells me that the FA are bound to do likewise, but if Villa do it first, it might lower the total amount. Then he adds: 'But I am going to give you the money back somehow.' If you ever hear of a player being fined two weeks' wages, don't assume that money won't find its way back into their bank account.

He does it because he likes me. He likes players with a bit of showmanship, a bit of swagger. He can't suffer dead-end Charlies walking around Bodymoor Heath with their head down.

Ron keeps me in the side for Saturday's game at Old Trafford. He asks me to do the team talk in the dressing room beforehand. I tell the players that deep down a lot of the United players don't think they're that good. I am not sure I believe what I am saying. Finally, Ferguson has United challenging for the title. They are a point behind Leeds with two games in hand.

As we assemble in the tunnel, Ferguson looks me up and down and says: 'How are you, old man?' Written down like this, it sounds an ordinary enough greeting, but the tone in his voice was cold and hard. The emphasis was on the words 'old man'. There was no twinkle in his eye. There is only one way to respond: 'I will show you how fucking old I am.'

When we win the toss, we decide to put United off their stride by defending the Stretford End in the first half, which is not how they like it. Elaine had come up to watch, and as I go over to the goal, I'm given a standing ovation. I have heard nothing like it in my career. I'm close to tears.

On the pitch, the players, like their manager, are considerably less friendly. Soon enough, United are awarded a corner. I'm making to throw the ball to a United player when Brian McClair glares at me, shouting: 'Give me the fucking ball.' As the corner is about to be taken, I tell Sean Teale, who is at the near post, to stand in front of Mark Hughes. Mark turns to me and says: 'What's the problem, Les? Can't you handle it on your own?'

Villa are pummelled. Old Trafford can be a very quiet stadium until United score. Then you are overwhelmed by a crescendo of noise. The sound swallows me up when

Hughes scores a few minutes after the interval. I can't hear myself think.

When United are in this kind of mood, one goal to the good, it is no longer about football: it becomes about survival. I play as well as I have ever done, and we lose 1–0. It ought to have been an absolute rout. When he comes into the dressing room, Ron says: 'I suppose you're fucking happy with that?' What he means is that some of his players might think a 1–0 defeat at Old Trafford isn't that bad. He wants to disabuse them of that notion.

Elaine and I drive straight back to Chingford. We stop at Keele services, and some United fans recognise me. We are surrounded. They all ask: 'Why did you leave?'

'Because I was told to go.'

There are so many autograph books and pieces of paper thrust our way that it takes twenty-five minutes to go from the service station to the car.

My time as one of Ron Atkinson's players is about to draw to a close. I am summoned to an FA tribunal at Lancaster Gate. Jim Barron rings me the night before to wish me luck, but nobody from the club accompanies me to London. I feel abandoned.

I meet Gordon Taylor, the head of my union, the Professional Footballers' Association, for a cup of coffee at the Royal Lancaster Hotel. He will be handling my defence. Gordon wants me to enter a not-guilty plea, but I have seen the footage – it has even been on *News at Ten*. I know I'm guilty. There's no escaping from it.

I sit down in front of a three-man panel, all of whom look old enough to have waved the *Titanic* off on its maiden voyage. I put my case and am then ushered out of the room, while they have a conference to discuss the evidence against me. They probably have a cup of tea, a slice of Manor House cake and a bet on the 3.30 at Southwell. It's a pretty open-and-shut case.

When I'm summoned back into the room, it's to be told that I will be fined £2,000 and banned for four matches. It's the ban that really unnerves me. I point out that George Courtney confirmed I had not sworn at him. I explain that in a fifteen-year career, I have been booked just three times and never sent off.

I also stress the consequences the ban will have on me. I'm thirty-four, and Aston Villa have a goalkeeper of Nigel Spink's quality in reserve. Four games would give Nigel ample opportunity to cement his place. These two facts mean that my career at Villa could be over if the ban were to be imposed.

That is exactly what happens. What I don't tell the commission is that the Villa chairman, Doug Ellis, who is on a number of FA boards and believes the corridors of power are his natural home, sees my actions as an embarrassment. The Villa board wants me gone. The FA imposes the ban, and off I go.

Hello, You're Through to Les Sealey

I am in the studios of Mercia Sound, the home of 'Today's Best Mix of Music', as it says on the mug of tea in my hand. I'm here to talk about my specialist chosen subject: 'The Life and Times of Leslie Jesse Sealey'. More specifically, I am here to talk about why I have come back to Coventry City.

Stuart Linnell, the sports editor, is opposite me. I never do interviews. I haven't since somebody at the *Coventry Evening Telegraph* turned me over soon after I first joined nearly twenty years ago. I'd been chatty and positive, said a couple of sentences about Gordon Milne not trusting me, and those were the lines they chose for their back-page headline. I had to apologise over and over again. To everybody. From then on, I've always said no.

But I've known Stuart for years. I'll be in safe hands. I used to offer him some of the jackets and other clobber that came my way when I was last at Coventry. He never seemed that keen. On go the headphones.

'Our first caller is Alan from Binley. What do you want to know from Les?'

'You know your last game for us, against West Ham, in 1983? Did you let in the goals deliberately?'

'No, of course I didn't.'

'But you seemed to celebrate at the end. We had lost, and West Ham are your team, aren't they?'

Another caller asks how I could have the nerve to come back after 'walking out of Coventry nine years ago'. I reply that I didn't walk out; my contract was up, and for the record, I have never deliberately let in a goal, not even against West Ham. I did punch the air on the final whistle because I was sick of the club's lack of ambition and delighted I wouldn't be playing for them again – or so I thought. I was amazed by the way Coventry had allowed eight players, including me, Mark Hateley, Gary Gillespie and Danny Thomas, to be out of contract in the same summer. Coventry had lost a fortune backing Jimmy Hill's ventures in America, and this was the price.

'But didn't you say the best thing about Coventry was the road out of it? You literally said that, didn't you? Literally. It was on the back of the *Telegraph*.'

'That was a joke. I am allowed to make the odd joke, you

know. And I'm coming back because I really love the club. It gave me my first break in the game, and I want to help Coventry and its fans avoid relegation. That's why I'm back.'

As the programme went to an ad break for Ford of Warwick, I asked where they had got these callers from. I told Stuart I usually avoided doing any interviews, and after this I wouldn't be rushing to do any more.

Eventually, the calls became more positive, but the whole tone of the programme seemed to be very anti-Les Sealey. I told the listeners that I didn't care how hard the fans booed me, I just wanted them to fill the ground and help Coventry avoid relegation.

When it became clear that Aston Villa no longer wanted me, I had seven offers to go out on loan. One was from Coventry, where I knew that I was absolutely hated because of how I'd left in 1983. Whenever I went back to Highfield Road with Luton or Manchester United, I was booed. Relentlessly. Why did I go back? Because I knew I would play.

Coventry were, as usual, just above the relegation zone. They had sacked their manager, Terry Butcher, in January 1992, and Don Howe, who had managed Arsenal and been Bobby Robson's assistant with England, was in charge until the end of the season. Their keeper, Steve Ogrizovic, had been injured on the training ground and they needed a stand-in quickly.

They had an on-loan keeper, Paul Heald, who'd been brought in from Leyton Orient, but I knew the club didn't rate him. This gave me quite a big bargaining chip. I negotiated an £8,000 bonus if Coventry stayed in the First Division and qualified for the newly formed Premier League.

On Saturday, 4 April 1992, I walk out at Highfield Road for my first game for Coventry in nine years. My name is read out to a crescendo of boos. I walk over to my goal to hear: 'Fuck off, Sealey.' A few coins land in the goalmouth. This is from the home support.

We lose 1–0, though I think I've played bloody well. I was still being booed when I went down the tunnel – 'Howled Down', as the headline in the *Coventry Evening Telegraph* put it.

In midweek, we play my old friends from Sheffield Wednesday. My last two games against them nearly cost me my leg and did cost me my place at Aston Villa. Now they are third in the table, while Coventry have won one match in two months and are a single place above the relegation zone.

After half an hour, the ball is cracked at me from about four yards. I stick an arm out, and it hits my wrist and bounces away. From behind the goal at Highfield Road, it looks like a wonder save, the kind that makes you shake your head in disbelief. As I get up to face the corner, I think the save was a combination of instinct and luck.

The mood of the crowd changes discernibly. The booing every time I touch the ball begins to fade away, and I'm even cheered when I make another, simpler save. The game finishes in a goalless draw. We are now six points clear of Luton, who are in the last relegation place.

It may have been because he thought he was suddenly under threat, but Steve Ogrizovic recovers more quickly than expected and declares himself fit for Saturday's game at Notts County. Don Howe tells me that Steve is the first-choice keeper and that he has no real option but to play him. I am only on loan.

Coventry lose 1–0 at Meadow Lane. The atmosphere in the dressing room is as silent and sullen as any I've known. We are still six points clear of Luton, but they have a game in hand.

What astonishes me is that the team haven't been out together all season. They don't socialise at all. I decide to organise a night out at a jazz club in Leamington Spa. Everyone is invited: the backroom staff, the apprentices, the players. Thirty-eight professionals walk in, and we put a glass in the middle of the table, fill it with ten- and twenty-pound notes and ask the owner to keep taking the money out until it's all gone. We end up drinking champagne cocktails at two in the morning, with our striker Robert Rosario dancing on the stage.

Suddenly, there's some laughter at the training ground. We may still be struggling but we're not bitching at each other.

I don't play another game for Coventry, but I reckon that night in Leamington helped keep them up. Coventry needed just a point from their final game, which was at Aston Villa of all places, to save themselves again and relegate Luton, managed by David Pleat, who took me from Highfield Road nine long years ago. We lose, but so do Luton, and there's another great escape to celebrate.

As I'm getting on the coach at Villa Park, Don Howe comes over and shakes my hand. 'Les, I didn't know what I was fucking getting when I signed you. A lot of what I've heard about you is bollocks. You'll do for me. You're my type.'

In the summer of 1992, I am back at Bodymoor Heath, but there's no chance I'll be staying at Aston Villa. Ron Atkinson has signed Mark Bosnich, who played a bit at Manchester United before going back to Australia. He's number two to Nigel Spink. He is twenty. I am thirty-four. I will not be getting a game.

However, as the 1992/3 Premier League season begins, one that will see Aston Villa and Manchester United fighting it out for the title, I am still pounding the motorways of the Midlands. I have been loaned out to Birmingham City. Their manager is Terry Cooper, who won just about everything at Leeds under Don Revie and has got Birmingham promoted to the Second Division. The birth of the Premier League has meant the Second Division has now been renamed the First Division.

We actually begin well, and when Birmingham beat

Southend at St Andrew's, we are second in the table. That's as far as it goes. The Kumar family own the club, and they have a lot of money tied up in the Bank of Credit and Commerce International, which is based in Karachi. BCCI has been lending large sums of money to people who, to put it bluntly, don't seem to exist. The Kumars go bust, and they take Birmingham City with them.

By November, the club is in administration and up for sale. By New Year's Day, Birmingham have won one match in four months and are a point off the relegation zone. They are not just the worst club I have ever played for, Birmingham have comfortably the worst team spirit I have ever come across.

The most toxic combination in a dressing room is one of apathy and fear. There are players who know they are not good enough, know there is nothing they can do to change their situation and who dread being exposed every Saturday after relentless bloody Saturday. At Birmingham, I see it every time I glance around.

I initially agreed to do a month, and it crawls by like a wounded animal. I'm asked to do another month. I say yes. I do so because I feel sorry for Terry Cooper. He is a good manager, but he needs to clear players out and bring his own people in. However, Birmingham have no money, can barely pay the wage bill. Along with everybody else at the club, he is trapped.

I'm living back in London and driving up to Birmingham

to train twice a week. Terry has also taken David Speedie on loan from Southampton to try to shore things up in attack. Speedie had played for Kenny Dalglish at Liverpool and Blackburn. He doesn't score a goal at Birmingham.

One Friday morning, the day before my loan period at St Andrew's was officially due to expire, I was lying on the settee in my underpants drinking a cup of coffee, while Elaine hoovered around me. The phone rang. I picked it up, and a Scottish voice on the other end said: 'How's the ugliest goalie in the world doing?' I struggled to place the accent. I thought it was Jim Leighton ringing. I knew he hadn't been enjoying his time at Dundee and might have wanted a chat, as goalkeepers do.

Then the voice went on, and I realised who it was. It was him. He was offering me a way back to Manchester United. I told Alex Ferguson I had six months left on my contract with Aston Villa. If he rang Ron Atkinson, he would let me go on a free transfer. 'I'll see you at the Cliff then,' said Ferguson.

I later found out why Ferguson wanted me back at Old Trafford: he thought I was lucky. Manchester United were closing in on their first league title since 1967. Perhaps he wanted lucky people around him.

The Lion and
the Unicorn

I'm on the bus, and it's almost ready to set off for the last game of the season. The engine's running. Tomorrow we wrap everything up in London – well, Wimbledon at Selhurst Park actually, but it's close enough for one or two of the lads to be talking about slipping out into the night to celebrate in the capital afterwards.

There is so much worth drinking to. On Sunday night, Manchester United became champions of England for the first time since I was kicking a ball outside Fort Vallance. We didn't even play. Aston Villa had to beat Oldham to keep the race open, and they lost.

Everyone had piled round to Steve Bruce's house to celebrate. Some of the lads left when dawn was breaking over

Cheshire. That evening, we played Blackburn at Old Trafford, and eleven hungover men won, 3–1.

All week there has been this fuzzy glow around the Cliff. I can sense it, and I've only been watching from the wings. I can't imagine how the manager feels. When I first met Alex Ferguson three years ago, he was on the brink of the sack, on the edge of forever imagining what might have been. Now he's done what no manager since Matt Busby has been able to achieve at Old Trafford. He's won his greatest battle.

Bryan Robson has been walking around with a dazed grin on his face. This meant more to him even than to Ferguson. Robbo came to Old Trafford in 1981, and for the next twelve years the best footballer in England saw Liverpool, Everton and then Arsenal dominate the league. Now it's his turn.

I didn't break open the booze, though yesterday evening I joined Paul Parker in the Unicorn, a nice pub in Wilmslow. I like Paul. He's from east London – Hornchurch. We talked about the kids, where we would go in the summer – Spain probably – and what the future might hold. I nursed my brandy; he had a couple of pints.

The manager is walking down the bus, which is full of bubble and chatter. He's like a teacher on a school trip, making sure we haven't left Tomkins in the toilets. When he gets to where Paul's sitting, he spins round, slaps him round the head and hisses: 'Don't go in the Unicorn.' He then turns to me and clips me too, before walking back to the front of the bus.

I once watched a *Panorama* documentary about Ceaușescu's Romania. Half the population were paid by the secret police to spy on the other half. It was like being a Manchester United player. Ferguson's network of informants are everywhere. All they need is a pair of eyes and a phone. You cannot escape.

Some of the drinking is unofficially sanctioned. After every away game, we'll be dropped off at the Four Seasons hotel near Manchester Airport, which has a bar called Mulligan's. If there's no midweek game, you can find us in Alderley Edge. We would start off in a wine bar and then finish up in a nightclub called Yesterdays.

There's actually more drinking at United now than there was when I was here in 1990, and I can understand why. The squad is much more united than it was three years ago, and there's a lot of success to celebrate. The pressure can get bottled up, and you need a release. Drinking gels teams together. When Everton were dominant in the mid-1980s, they would go out all the time – and if you didn't, you were in big trouble. Luton, who were very successful for such a small club, had a very healthy social scene. I didn't get involved as much in the off-field activities at Aston Villa because I lived in London, but I do know that Ron Atkinson used to make them go out. He wanted them to bond, and if I ever became a manager, I would do the same.

Sometimes, the rules change. If the game is on a Saturday, we're not allowed to go out on Thursday or Friday. The following April, we beat Liverpool on a Wednesday night at Old Trafford, and Roy Keane, Lee Sharpe and Gary Pallister went out straight after the game. We were at Blackburn on the Saturday evening. Nothing was said in training or at the team meeting on Friday. We went to Ewood Park and lost 2–0, which cut our lead to three points. Straight after the game, the manager informed the three players that he had known all along they had been out after the Liverpool game, and because of that they would each be fined a week's wages. Then he turned to the rest of us: 'Right, the season's getting critical. I don't want to hear reports of any of you going out at any time. That includes restaurants, by the way.'

With a little nervous laugh, Dion Dublin said: 'Gaffer, I've promised to take my wife out. You're not really saying we can't go and eat Italian food?'

'Aye, that's precisely what I am saying. You can always cook her something.'

The Garden Party

I am at one of Manchester United's big social events of the year: the Captain's Barbecue. When we go out as a team, the Captain's Barbecue is the only time we're encouraged to take the wives. It's a proper do.

We have all gathered at Bryan Robson's house, which looks like something from the pages of *Cheshire Life*. I don't think Robbo's going to flip the burgers; people have been brought in to do the cooking. There's an actual bar.

Paul Ince has just parked up in his Mercedes. I walk over and say: 'I hope you've locked your glove compartment.'

His wife Claire gives me a blank look. Paul laughs: 'Fuck off, Sealey.'

Towards the end of last season, I'd come to the Cliff without my wallet and asked Paul if he could lend me a tenner to get some petrol. He told me there might be some money in his car. I went over to the Mercedes, which was unlocked, and opened the glove compartment. It was stuffed full of ten-, twenty- and fifty-pound notes. I counted them out on the passenger seat. They came to £1,800. I put a ten-pound note in one of the pockets of my tracksuit, folded the rest up and put them in the other pocket.

The next day, I walked over to him in the dressing room, proffering a ten-pound note in my hand.

'Oh, thanks.'

'By the way, Paul, are you missing anything?'

'No, not especially.'

I handed over the bundle of notes. 'You mean you haven't noticed this little lot has gone walkabouts?'

He laughed. 'Sealey, you wanker.'

Paul is rather lucky to be going to the barbecue. He is rather lucky to still be a Manchester United player, given what happened at Norwich. If it had been anyone else, he would have been sacked.

In April, we had a Monday-night match at Carrow Road. United went into it third in the table. Norwich were ahead of us, and Aston Villa were four points clear at the top. Games are running out. We probably have to win. We dare not lose.

We are sensational. After twenty-one minutes, we are three goals up: Giggs, Kanchelskis and Cantona. Paul made Eric's goal with a driving run through the middle and a pass that went straight to Cantona's feet. All of it done at the speed of an athlete running the 400 metres.

Mark Robins, who plays for Norwich now, pulls one back, and suddenly there's a bit of tension in the night air. Once more, Paul surges through the centre of the pitch, and there's a chance he can find Cantona once more and help put the game to bed. He doesn't. He takes one touch too many and stumbles.

On the bench, the manager goes berserk, turns to the physio, Jim McGregor, and yells: 'Get Ince's number, he's bloody coming off for that.' As Jim fumbles around looking for the number eight, the manager changes his mind. United hold on to win, 3–1. We are a point behind Villa with a better goal difference.

As the players clatter down the corridor and into the away dressing room, Ferguson is waiting by the door. As each red shirt comes in, he pats them on the shoulder. The words 'well done son', and 'great game' keep repeating. Then Paul comes in, and Ferguson turns to him: 'I'm disappointed in you, Ince. When the fuck are you going to learn to look up when you're on a run?'

Given that he's been involved in one of the goals of Manchester United's season, Paul looks like he's just been slapped. He lunges for his manager, who stands his ground. The dressing room is divided by a treatment table. On one side of it, Paul is being held back by four of his teammates, screaming: 'If that's what you think, why don't you sell me, you cunt? Go on then, fucking sell me. You haven't got the fucking bottle, have you?'

On the other side, Ferguson is standing bolt upright,

gripping the table, refusing to take a step back. They glare at each other, two bulls fighting for control of the herd. Nobody moves. Nobody breathes.

Second by imperceptible second, the crisis starts to deflate. Steve Bruce says: 'Can I remind everyone in this room that we have just beaten Norwich 3–1?' People start disappearing towards the showers. Paul sits down. The manager leaves to give his press conference.

A few days later, Ferguson is sitting in his office at the Cliff when he sees the barrel of a rifle poking through the gap in the door, which slowly swings open. There, pointing a double-barrelled shotgun straight at Ferguson's chest, is Paul.

They look straight into each other's eyes.

'Don't worry, gaffer,' Paul smiles. 'It's not loaded.'

I don't even know if the gun was real, but it broke the ice. Paul stayed in the team, and Manchester United won the championship. Paul got away with it because he was too good to drop. He could answer back. Likewise with Peter Schmeichel. Their ability gave them some protection.

The same went for Eric Cantona, although there was never a row between the manager and Eric in front of the players. The club employed an interpreter for Eric and Andrei Kanchelskis called George Scanlan, who was a professor at Liverpool University and spoke fluent French and Russian. He was the official interpreter for the Soviet Union's football team during the 1966 World Cup. If the manager wanted to make a specific point to either of them or give them a bit of a bollocking, they would be taken into a side room with the Prof, and if the manager began shouting, George would raise his voice with him. You could just make out a stream of words you couldn't understand, while someone behind you would say: 'What's French for "fuck off"?'

Paul Parker is walking around the garden on his phone. He was one of the first at the club to get a mobile, and he has a home phone that lights up when there's a call waiting. He came to the party in a Saab 900 convertible, wearing an Armani suit. Very stylish. Every time United earn a win bonus, I say to him: 'Another jacket, Paul?' His wife sent him out the other day to get their daughter, Georgie, a bike. He came back with one. He also came back with £1,500 worth of clothes.

When I first went to United, that kind of behaviour would lead to loud whispers in the dressing room: 'He must have won on the horses,' or 'Where's the money coming from?' Nobody wonders where the money comes from now. It's being pumped into Old Trafford via pipelines.

Mark Hughes is having a place built for himself in the countryside, not far from Mottram Hall, which is the hotel United use for team meetings and golf days. He grew up in a village in North Wales, and I don't suppose it was a roses-round-the-door kind of village. When he was a boy, that was probably the rural life he imagined for himself, and now he can live it. He's always loved cars, sports cars in particular, but now he's gone and got himself a Range

Rover to join the Barbour-jacket brigade. The other day we presented him with a pair of green wellies, and in the dressing room he's known as the Duke of Mottram.

You are treated differently at Manchester United. Once, not long after the 1990 FA Cup final, I went clothes shopping in Wilmslow. It was a place where a lot of the players went. The owner asked if he could have his photo taken with me. Naturally, I said yes, and we had a good chat about football. He then said the clothes would cost £500. Fair enough, you might think, but the price tags on the clothes added up to £1,100.

I once read an article about Graeme Souness, who remarked that when he was playing in Italy for Sampdoria, he had to pay for everything. When he was captaining Liverpool to European Cups and league titles, just about everything that came his way was gratis. That's how it is when you're top dog.

One thing I do know is that all the footballers in Robbo's garden will always be known as Manchester United players wherever they go and whatever they do. There was something on the television about Sammy McIlroy recently. He's the manager of Macclesfield, but he kept being referred to as 'the former Manchester United footballer'. Sammy hasn't been a player at Old Trafford since 1982. He played for seven clubs after leaving, including Stoke and Manchester City, but he will always be 'ex-Manchester United'. The club never leaves you; it is never allowed to.

Night Flight

It must be, what, two in the morning? Probably later. I have no idea where we are or what's below us. Greece? Italy? The Alps?

I can hear the pulse of the engines, but the only voices are at the front of the plane. The directors of Manchester United are probably discussing how many millions they have lost or, more accurately, how many millions we have lost them. One of the directors, an entrepreneur called Michael Edelson, is walking up and down the aisle of the plane, looking to his left and his right to see what we have on our tray tables. Edelson is not liked. He tells tales to the board, and this is not a time to be seen drinking alcohol. As he walks up and down the plane, everyone keeps shtum. This is no time for banter either.

Given we have thrown away a £14,000-a-man bonus for

reaching the group stages, there wasn't much conversation even before Edelson started prowling around. The trip has been an absolute fuck-up. It is the early hours of 4 November 1993, and United are out of the European Cup. It was the first time the club had been in the competition since 1969. We all knew what it meant.

When we get back, the papers will tell us that we were intimidated in Istanbul. I expect there will be a few stories about the violence meted out to us after the game; that we froze, and that was all Galatasaray required to go through. What they probably won't mention is how badly we played. Peter Schmeichel is in the seat behind me, dozing fitfully, waking up, yawning and then falling asleep again. But for him, Galatasaray would have won 2–0 rather than hold us to a goalless draw. They wouldn't have needed the away-goals rule to see them through. They won't be saying that this was a disaster made not in Istanbul but in the first leg in Manchester.*

That storm had come from nowhere. We beat Honvéd in the first round and then drew Galatasaray. Les Kershaw, who is United's chief scout, told us Galatasaray wouldn't give us any problems; they were the weakest team left in the tournament, while we were already seven points clear at the top of the Premier League. Nobby Stiles, who was

---

* In 1993–94 the Champions League consisted of two knockout rounds followed by a group stage. The top two in each group qualified for the semi-finals.

now United's youth-team coach, wasn't so sure. He told us they were not as bad as people were making out. The Turks would be difficult.

Kershaw told Nobby he was talking nonsense. 'We will coast it,' he said. That was the worst piece of foreign scouting since Neville Chamberlain came back from Munich declaring: 'Peace in our time.'

After twenty minutes at Old Trafford, it seemed Kershaw was right. The Turks couldn't cope with the noise of the stadium. They looked like boys, boys who had conceded two goals away to Manchester United with seventy long minutes ahead of them. Watching from the bench, the only question going through my mind was how deep their humiliation would become.

Then Galatasaray scored, a long-range shot that flew into the top corner past Peter Schmeichel. From that moment on, United fell apart. We didn't seem to know how to play. They equalised before half-time. I glanced across at the manager. The look on Alex Ferguson's face was one of total disbelief. There was anger etched deep into the corners of his mouth.

When we went down the tunnel at half-time, I thought to myself that what was coming would not be pleasant. Ferguson shut the door and ripped into the centre-halves. He blamed Schmeichel for the first goal, which seen through a goalkeeper's eyes had looked unsavable.

We responded to his threats by playing even worse. Galatasaray scored again to make it 3–2. They might have had a fourth and a fifth. With a few moments left, Eric Cantona appeared from nowhere to volley a cross into the net. To me, he seemed to have the movement of a ballet dancer and the precision of an engineer. Paul Ince hit the outside of the post in the closing seconds: 3–3.

Afterwards, Ferguson came into the dressing room and looked everyone up and down. 'You've got it all to do now.' After a pause, he shouted: 'And you'd better fucking do it!' Then he left.

As we gathered at Manchester Airport to fly to Istanbul for the second leg, the scouting department's view of the tie had changed. It was no longer going to be so easy. We were told to expect a 'hothouse atmosphere'. We were so convinced the Turks were going to poison us that we brought our own chef. When the England cricket team toured India or Pakistan, the players would live off corned beef and fried eggs. We were served something a little more sophisticated, and we also brought our own security guards to patrol the floor of the hotel we were booked into.

The scenes at Istanbul Airport were beyond our imaginings. We were jeered, we were jostled, we were threatened. I felt a shove in the back and heard a heavily accented voice saying: 'Fuck off to Manchester.' I spun round to confront him, a rolled-up copy of *Autotrader* brandished above my head. For half a second, we stared at each other with a mutual recognition of how ridiculous this was, before our security guards swept me and my teammates towards the exits.

The coach, a double-decker Volvo, provided no respite. No sooner were we on it than it was struck by a volley of stones. The players, who were all on the top deck, responded with two-fingered gestures and more. We did everything except drop our trousers, which only enraged them more. It was not something the club's marketing department would want on the end-of-season video. Another volley of stones came our way. The windows on the lower deck began to crack, and the manager and directors, who were below us, began yelling at the driver to 'get us out, get us out of here'. It was not exactly a getaway Steve McQueen would have recognised, because traffic in Istanbul moves at the speed of an especially lethargic glacier, enveloped not by snow and ice but by carbon monoxide fumes.

The hotel was a refuge. It was beautiful, serene, full of cool marble, lying on the banks of the Bosporus. We were told that under no circumstances should we attempt to leave it. A police launch patrolled back and forth along the waterfront.

I walked through the gardens to where the hotel met the city streets. The gate was locked and in front of it was a uniformed local security guard, a bear of a man, holding his baton like a rifle. I wasn't inclined to tell him that I felt like exploring.

As night fell, I stood on the balcony, watching the oil tankers grunting their way down the Bosporus, trying to work out if I was on the European side of the city or actually in Asia. It was never a problem I encountered when playing for Luton. Then I heard a muffled booming noise coming from the quayside below. It kept getting louder, and then I saw a lad, wearing a T-shirt and jeans, with a big bass drum strapped to his body. He was walking up and down the quay pounding the thing. 'Good luck if you plan to keep that up all night,' I thought. I closed the curtains.

Dawn was a long way over the horizon when my eyes opened. I could still hear the drum and walked out on to the balcony. There was a sharp, cold wind blowing, and the lad was marching much more slowly now beneath the street lamps. He seemed a little dishevelled. He looked up and smiled at me. I gave him a little wave. He was probably pleased by the fact he'd kept a Manchester United player awake. A little pre-match victory for Galatasaray. If he knew I had absolutely no chance of playing, he might have considered his work a little less valuable.

The next evening, the day before the match, I was fiddling with the TV remote, trying to find a film in English. Skipping the channels, I kept coming across different scenes but all featuring the same three actors in a variety of backdrops. Either these were different episodes of a soap opera or Turkish cinema had a recruitment problem.

Then came the pounding of the drum. The lad was wearing the same clothes, though they did look a little more worn. He had got his rhythm back, though. Two policemen approached him. He stopped and shrugged, holding his drumsticks stretched out in either hand. The policemen walked towards the boy. One drew his baton and sent it smashing into the boy's knees. The other cracked him over the back of his neck. He went straight down, his big drum smashing on the pavement. They took hold of his hands and dragged him away.

We were gathering in the foyer on the afternoon of the game when Gordon Milne walked in. He was the manager of Beşiktaş, Galatasaray's great cross-city rivals. Coventry felt very far away to both of us.

He had come to brief Alex Ferguson on what to expect. I stopped him and asked him how he thought we'd do. 'The result they got at Old Trafford was as good as they could possibly have hoped for. It was beyond their dreams. That was the best I have ever seen them play, and I've been here seven years. You can certainly play better.' As he moved away, he turned and gave me the smile of someone who knows he understands things far better than you do. 'You'll win, 4–0.'

We don't have a bloody shot on target.

The noise at the Ali Sami Yen stadium is overwhelming. I can't hear what anybody else on the bench is saying. I can't hear Ferguson yelling out his instructions. The air tastes of the smoke from the flares.

We have to score. Galatasaray's only aim is to block us. It's like Gallipoli. If the Turks had met the British and

Australians in open battle when we invaded in 1915, we would have knocked Turkey out of the war. But they didn't. They dug in, put their machine guns behind sandbags and picked us off. That's what they are doing in the Ali Sami Yen: they are digging in and picking us off.

When it's all over and Galatasaray have got the goalless draw they need, all hell breaks loose. Eric Cantona has worked himself into a frenzy about the Turks' time-wasting and fouling, enough to get himself sent off on the final whistle, when he accuses the referee, who is from Switzerland, of taking money. I don't think he was bent. He looked a frightened man. Like the rest of us, I don't think he could cope with the noise, the smoke and the crowd. I don't think he wanted to make any decision that would prevent him from getting away from the Ali Sami Yen safely. He blew the whistle exactly on ninety minutes.*

In the tunnel, Eric gets a policeman's truncheon on the back of his head. Bryan Robson spins round to intervene and is struck on the forearm by a riot shield. He needs four or five stitches.

The manager has gone to the press conference. Once

---

* The referee was Kurt Röthlisberger, who was later convicted of asking Grasshoppers Zürich for $600,000 to fix their Champions League fixture with Auxerre in October 1996. He told the club he would contact the Belarusian match referee on their behalf. Grasshoppers reported Röthlisberger to UEFA and won the game 3–1. Röthlisberger, who had already been suspended for three months for using an official FIFA referee's uniform to campaign for a seat in the Swiss parliament, was banned for life.

Eric has calmed down, there is a perfect silence in the dressing room. I mean total silence. Nobody speaks for twenty minutes. We just sit there, numb from the noise, the violence we have just seen and the result. Then somebody – Steve Bruce, because he's always rallying the troops – says: 'Shall we get changed and get on the bus?'

On the way to the airport the Turks don't give up. As the bus goes by, they scream and shout, they give us the finger, they take the piss. As we make our way along the dual carriageways of Istanbul, past what seems to be an endless array of car showrooms, there's no conversation at all. Even when you've lost, there's always some talk on the bus. Somebody might blurt out how gutted they feel or how shit the referee had been. They might even turn on someone in the seat next to them and say how shit they were. But as the suburbs of Istanbul slide by, nobody says a word. We are driven straight on to the runway, where the plane is waiting.

We're starting our descent into Manchester. All the orange street lights are stretched out below us. The houses are in darkness, waiting for dawn and for the paperboy to push the *Daily Mail* through the letterbox, which will tell them about their football club's journey to hell and back.

A few days later, we are on another bus, travelling through an area that's every bit as murderously hostile as the streets of Istanbul: Moss Side. Three days after returning home from Turkey, it's the Manchester derby.

The bus is being pelted not with stones or rocks but with packets of Turkish Delight. When we arrive at Maine Road, there are City fans wearing T-shirts with the slogan: 'Manchester United European Champions 1994'. The word 'Cancelled' is stamped across their chests.

When we go on the pitch to warm up, we are met by another volley of Turkish Delight. I can't imagine the profits the sweet shops of Moss Side must be raking in.

At half-time, City are two up. We seem unable to escape the memories of Istanbul, and on the way to the dressing room I'm expecting to witness the mother and father of all bollockings from Ferguson. Instead, he walks in and says very calmly: 'You are not out of this yet. You need to keep playing the way you are.'

We don't change our shape or our tactics. Instead of passing back to his goalkeeper, Michel Vonk passes straight to Eric Cantona, who scores. It is still 2–1 to Manchester City, but they are beaten. You can see it in their faces, the way they are running. Their legs and their power have gone. They are finished. Roy Keane scores, and then Eric gets his second.

It is one of the wins that will help make Manchester United champions again. Had we lost at Maine Road after what happened in Istanbul, we might have collapsed completely. The gulf in class in Manchester football is like that between Eton and Roughhouse Comprehensive.

When we were on the bus parading the Cup Winners'

Cup a few years back, we encountered a sky-blue Ford Capri, inside which was a Manchester City fan, wearing a sky-blue Manchester City shirt. We began jeering at him and waving the cup in his direction, and he looked up at us and then his head slumped forward on to the steering wheel. It must be hell to follow City now.

The Untouchables

It's January 1994. I am on the Manchester United team coach, returning from Sir Matt Busby's funeral.

I met him only once. I knew he had an office at Old Trafford, which long after he retired as manager was still a source of power at United. The power faded with age, but he continued to go to it if he had nothing else to do. One afternoon, when I was at a loose end, I searched it out, knocked on the door and turned the handle. He was behind his desk, just sitting there. There was an aura, almost a shimmering light around him. I felt like I was approaching an old Jedi knight.

'Hello, Les.' A soft Scottish burr highlighted one of his great traits: an ability to remember people's names. We'd never had a conversation before. Then he added: 'What have you come here for?'

And I didn't know. I hadn't planned out a conversation. I didn't really expect him to be in. I was flummoxed.

'I just wanted to know who was the best player you ever managed?'

'That's a very hard question, son. You want a player who has a bit of everything. Best had a bit of everything.'

'But if you had to pick just one name, who would it be?' I realised I was sounding like a twelve-year-old autograph hunter.

'Well, if I had to pick one, it would be Duncan Edwards.' He looked up at the ceiling, his eyes half closed. 'Had he lived, he would have become the greatest player in the world.'

As we get on the bus after the funeral, held at a modest Catholic church in Chorlton, the manager and his staff are, as usual, in the front. The players, in their club blazers, are fanned out behind them. Then the chairman, Martin Edwards, clambers aboard and begins searching for a seat. Nothing has been reserved for him, and nobody stands up and offers him theirs. He sits down, awkwardly, next to me and begins a conversation that is equally awkward. It's like talking to Prince Charles.

'Les, why do you think Alan Shearer opted to go to Blackburn instead of Manchester United?'

'I think it might be something to do with the extra three grand a week Blackburn are paying him, Mr Chairman.'

'But we are Manchester United.'

Although things have changed radically in the dressing room and on the pitch, the boardroom still imagines players will come to Old Trafford just because we are Manchester United. Blackburn and Newcastle think their money will talk louder than our name.

As we draw nearer to Old Trafford, Edwards leans over and says: 'Do you think we'll win the league?'

We are thirteen points clear of Blackburn. We have lost one game all season. There is nobody on that bus who is not totally convinced that United will win the Premier League. I have no idea why the chairman of the club needs my reassurance. Nevertheless, Blackburn and Newcastle do better in the media than us. There are people in the press out to get us.

Three days later, we play Norwich in the FA Cup. It's live on television, and Eric Cantona launches into a two-footed tackle on Jeremy Goss. Jimmy Hill is commentating for the BBC and has a go at Eric. He calls him 'despicable'.

The following morning, the manager gathers the team together. His first words are: 'I am losing control of this club. All contact with the media is banned. If I hear of anyone talking to the press, you will see the other side of me.'

Nobody speaks to the newspapers, not even Steve Bruce, who always gives interviews.

When United lose 2–0 at Blackburn in April, our lead is cut to three points, and we are portrayed as a team that is thuggish when we win and can't take it when we lose.

We gain the impression that the press want Blackburn to be champions. United winning the league in 1993 for the first time in twenty-six years had been a good story for them, but Blackburn winning it would be a better one. The last time they were league champions was in 1914 and the country was about to go to war with the Kaiser.

When we arrived for training, the papers would always be laid out alongside a pot of tea, coffee and biscuits, and every morning a few of us would go through them and take the piss out of the reports. If there was an article about anyone in the group, someone would laugh: 'Ain't that scandalous? Something should be done about him.' We didn't care what they wrote. We were top of the Premier League. We were untouchable.

Manchester United is the most competitive place I have ever worked at. It is the only club I have ever been to where nobody has feigned injury because they didn't fancy playing. When I was first here, the Old Trafford crowd could be vicious. They expected mistakes, they looked for them, and when they happened, they howled the players down. Some of them couldn't handle it. You would hear them mentioned in the dressing room by the backroom staff. Names like Garry Birtles, Neil Webb, Danny Wallace. Very good players everywhere else, but not at Old Trafford. You could see it in their faces. When they were dropped, they seemed quite pleased they weren't playing, pleased to be missing.

Now when a game kicks off, Old Trafford waits, not for mistakes made by a red shirt but for the opposition to be ripped apart. Swindon conceded four, Leicester and Sheffield Wednesday five. Everyone wants to play. I have sometimes sat on the bench injured because I didn't want to lose my place as United's reserve goalkeeper.

The club is so well-run it seems to operate on autopilot. There is very little analysis. Alex Ferguson never sits us down in a room to go through videos on what's gone right or, more rarely, what's gone wrong. He's always concentrating on finding the next player, moulding the team, making little adjustments.

Archie Knox is no longer his assistant. Just before the Cup Winners' Cup final, he signed a contract with Glasgow Rangers to become assistant to Walter Smith. Archie had been Ferguson's number two at Aberdeen, and when he came to Manchester, they shared a flat. After he left, Ferguson didn't speak to Knox for eighteen months. He kept saying he had only gone there 'for the money' – an extra two grand a month or something. They're friends again now, apparently, but they've taken their time about it.

Training is now in the hands of Brian Kidd, who is very sharp, very innovative, but when he's away the manager sometimes takes a session. When we see him coming over, the players all stifle big comedy yawns because Ferguson's training routines are so bloody boring. The training and the team talks are very low-key. There's no need to be technical when you've got the best players in the country, and that breeds an inner confidence.

We are at the Cliff. All the talk is about playing Liverpool. Although everyone is trying to mask it, there is plenty of tension in the air. Paul Ince is pacing the room. When some minion puts his head round the door, he shouts: 'Oi, you, where's my fucking coffee?'

Then Mark Hughes walks in. He is habitually the last to arrive. He looks around him and grins. 'Oh, it's Ruddock tomorrow. Great stuff.'

The nerves, the ones we all pretend aren't there, evaporate. We know we are going to win, and we do. Paul scores the only goal.

Villain

When I came back to Old Trafford in 1993, I had been away for eighteen months. There were two things that struck me immediately. The team itself – it was faster. There was speed throughout the midfield and up top. Andrei Kanchelskis drove down one flank and Ryan Giggs attacked the other. Players like Mike Phelan and Neil Webb had a lot of class but they didn't have pace, and that's why they had been forced out. Alex Ferguson had made up his mind about Phelan after the debacle in Istanbul.

The other thing was that at every club I've ever been to, I've looked at the first-choice keeper and thought: 'You are catchable.' When I saw Peter Schmeichel, I knew immediately he wasn't. He had no weakness that I could see. Unless something happened to him, I would be watching from the bench. He was the best goalkeeper I had ever seen. Yet

Ferguson would needle him, criticise him in a way he never would with Eric Cantona. Peter and Eric room together and would often while away the time playing backgammon. Peter's interesting like that; he's also a very skilful piano player, and when he plays, any false notes irritate him. He wants perfection.

Peter is a man apart at Manchester United. He is not particularly liked. I don't think many at Old Trafford are close to him; he is just respected for what he does. Nobody, incidentally, is allowed to touch his gloves. However, when we go to Anfield, we lose a three-goal lead to draw 3–3. The dressing room is murderous, and the manager lays into Peter. He criticises his kicking, his placement and even his basic ability as a goalkeeper. Peter answers back and tells him to 'fuck off' four times.

I'm not surprised Peter cracks, because the manager is relentless with him. He tells him he is finished at Manchester United, and we all think that is it. There is silence in the dressing room, because none of us can recall Ferguson changing his mind once he has announced something.

Before the bus leaves, we stand around in little clumps. I try to think what the next games are, because I'll be playing. I ask Paul Ince: 'Sheffield United away in the FA Cup, then League Cup against Portsmouth. Nothing you can't handle. You've got the bottle, Sealey. You'll be up for it.'

I don't feel remotely ready. I haven't played all season and have barely been playing in the reserves. I could help knock United out of two cup competitions in a week. It's not about bottle. You could grab ten people from Lou Macari's chip shop outside the ground or the Trafford Arms and they would have the bottle. They just wouldn't be any good.

Sidling up to Steve Bruce, I say: 'Do you think he'll go through with it? Do you think he'll finish with Peter?'

'Nah. He's too important. Now if it was Denis . . .'

And we both burst out laughing because the thought of Denis Irwin telling Ferguson to fuck off four times is too ridiculous for words.

The next day, the manager called Peter in to fire him. He told him he could not have his authority challenged in front of the players. If he allowed it, he'd be finished. Twenty-four hours later, he changed his mind. Peter has made some phenomenal saves over the past two seasons, which are taken for granted by the management. Why would you toss away one of your best assets just because of an argument? For the first time any of us can remember, Ferguson backed down.

Peter played in both cup games. That said something, because they were games where he might have been left out just to make a point. The manager decided it was a point not worth making.

We beat Sheffield United at Bramall Lane, but the League Cup quarter-final is different. Portsmouth are a division below us and mid-table. We are top of the Premier League by a very long way. Towards the end of the game, Peter parries a shot at his near post, but the rebound goes straight to Paul Walsh, who equalises. Peter hammers the pitch with his glove. In public the manager blames the forwards – Giggs and Cantona – for not finishing Portsmouth off. We win the replay.

A month later, we lost 1–0 to Wimbledon at Selhurst Park. Blackburn had lost earlier in the day at Southampton, and this had been a chance to extend our lead, a chance we had just blown. Ferguson came over to Peter and said: 'I don't know if I'm going to pick you next week. I've had enough of this. You're making mistakes every fucking week.'

The next week was the Manchester derby at Old Trafford. Of course, Peter was picked. United won 2–0. We won five of our last six games – including the FA Cup final against Chelsea – and drew the other. Peter conceded just one goal.

We didn't win the Treble. We lost the League Cup final to Aston Villa, which gave Ron Atkinson some revenge for losing out on the title the year before. It was my fourth and last final for Manchester United. Just like my first, in 1990, I hadn't expected to play, but a fortnight prior to the final, we'd faced Charlton in the FA Cup at Old Trafford. A minute before half-time, Peter comes tearing out of his area and upends the Charlton forward, Kim Grant, who is going through on goal. The result is a red card. Paul Parker comes off, and I come on for what will be my last appearance at Old Trafford as a United player. Although we have ten men, it's still too many for Charlton. Hughes and Kanchelskis ensure we win, 3–1.

It's only in the players' lounge that I realise I'm a certainty to play in the League Cup final. I'm excited, but anxious because I've had so little football. I train like a dog, but it's not the same as playing. I know it's not the same, and so do the coaching staff. In 1990, I'd had two full games against Queens Park Rangers and Aston Villa. This time, I've had forty-six minutes against a lower-division team.

The thing about Peter is that he always wants to play, whatever the state of the season, whatever the opposition. In October, we were at home to Leicester in the League Cup. Before kick-off, I was having a piss in one of the urinals when the manager came over to use the facilities. As he stood next to me, he said: 'I was going to play you tonight, but you know what that fucker Schmeichel's like when you ask him to stand down. I'm sorry.'

On the Wednesday after the Charlton tie, we're playing Sheffield Wednesday at Old Trafford. At half-time United are 4–0 up, and as we go down the tunnel, the manager says to me: 'I'm going to put you on for the second half.'

When he explains the decision to Peter, there's another row. Peter stands up: 'I'm not happy with that. I'm not fucking happy with that.' Suddenly, this looks like another argument that is going to spiral completely out of control. Before it does, Ferguson backs down and mumbles an apology to me. The second half is an irrelevance. We score another and win 5–0.

As I leave the dressing room, the manager taps me on the shoulder. 'I've got to keep him happy. Don't worry, I'll make sure you get a reserve game.'

Since I am United's reserve goalkeeper, you might think it's pretty automatic that I'd play those games. The reality is a little more complex. Gary Walsh, who might have played in the Cup Winners' Cup final before Ferguson took that wild gamble on me, is still at the club, which is looking to sell him. However, if they want to sell Gary, they have to play him in the reserve fixtures so scouts can assess his form. I was told I could have the next reserve game: Leeds at home. We won 7–0, and apart from a single shot, I simply stood and watched.

When I watch the League Cup final back on television, I hear Brian Moore say: 'Les Sealey, he won't lack for confidence.' Well, I can tell you, Brian, that this was something I did lack. When you haven't started a first-team game in a year, you need to get a feel of the ball. You need to judge its speed, the way it dips for a cross.

United were so dominant in the final that I didn't touch the ball until the game was twenty-two minutes old. Steve Staunton put in a corner that looked like it might float into the far corner. Back-pedalling, I tipped it over. Until then, my work had consisted of four back-passes.

Four minutes later, Aston Villa score. Dalian Atkinson

is put through on goal, with Steve Bruce at his heels. He takes two touches and jabs it past me. Had I been more match fit, I might have reacted just that fraction quicker and closed Atkinson down. As we kick off, a goal down, I think: 'Schmeichel, you absolute fucker.'

Almost right on full-time we are trailing 2–1, when Andrei Kanchelskis handles Atkinson's shot on the line. He is sent off, although I think Andrei deserves just a booking, and Villa are awarded a penalty. Dean Saunders smashes it straight down the middle of the goal as I go to my left. It is the last shot aimed at me as a Manchester United player.

Ferguson was more relaxed than when we lost the League Cup to Sheffield Wednesday three years ago. Winning the league last season has taken so much pressure off him that he can stand and chat with Ron Atkinson. In defeat. Not so long ago, he would have been physically unable to do that.

He makes an exception for Mark Bosnich, though. When they pass in the corridor, the manager just stares at him, eyes full of venom. Bosnich had played for Manchester United once as a teenager in April 1990, just before the FA Cup final. He kept a clean sheet against Wimbledon, but he was Australian, on a student visa, and when he returned home, United could not obtain a work permit for him.

Two years later, Mark married an English girl, which meant he didn't need a work permit. Someone told Ron Atkinson, who took him to Aston Villa before United could react. In Villa's semi-final against Tranmere, Mark had saved three penalties in the shoot-out.

Ferguson could not stomach being outfoxed. He didn't blame Atkinson, but he did blame Mark for not informing United that his circumstances had changed. He even blamed Mark's parents for not telling him. As Mark disappears down the corridor with his winner's medal, the glare follows him.*

---

* His dislike of Mark Bosnich did not stop Sir Alex Ferguson signing him in 1999 as a replacement for Peter Schmeichel. It was a decision Ferguson regretted almost immediately, describing Bosnich as 'a terrible professional'.

A Gardener's World

Very soon it was spring 1994. A spring in which we were confident we would become the first Manchester United side to win the league and FA Cup Double. As the tension around the club began to ease, Paul Ince said to me after training: 'Do you want to come round mine and watch some racing?'

Of course, I said yes. As the reserve goalkeeper, I accept every invitation that comes my way. And I like Paul. When he's being watched, he feels as though he has to act like Reggie Kray, but in close company he is softer, warmer and funnier than he cares to pretend. Especially when he's with his family.

He had bought his wife a Mercedes 380SL. A sports car, a thing of beauty. It cost him £58,000. She had just started driving it then Claire scratched it down one side. She looked at the dent and waited for her husband to come home. No sooner had the key turned in the lock than she tried to explain about the car. Paul marched over to have a look, marched back and said: 'Darling, it is only a car. We will have it repainted.' He gave her a hug. He adores his family.

Paul lives right in the stockbroker belt. He's got a doctor on one side of him and a solicitor on the other. God knows what they make of the language that comes from the house in the middle. When Paul arrived at Manchester from West Ham, Steve Bruce put him in touch with a friend of his, who's an estate agent. He was shown around this beautiful house in Bramhall. He soon became impatient and said: 'I like it. What's the dough?' When he was told it was on sale for £330,000, he turned to the club's solicitor, who was with him, and said: 'I'll take it. You deal with it,' and left.

The estate agent phoned Paul later and told him: 'You do know you are allowed to negotiate on property?' The agent managed to get the price reduced by £45,000 because it was a cash sale. Paul thought he was a genius.

It was significant that Paul had asked if I wanted to watch horse racing. This might be Manchester United's most successful team for a quarter of a century, but the players don't tend to watch football. If it's on in the pub, they might glance up at the screen, but as for sitting down, enjoying a match and talking about it afterwards, it's not something that interests them.

The telly's on, and we're sitting in some big furniture while Paul looks through the *Racing Post*.

'What are you going to be when you grow up?' I ask him. England have failed to qualify for the World Cup in America. Terry Venables has replaced Graham Taylor as manager and plenty of futures are being considered.

'I want to captain England. I want to be the first black England captain.'

'But you've already captained England. You lost to the USA. At football. The bloody Yanks. They're not going to ask you back after that.'

Paul shoots me the kind of stare that he dishes out during games. 'It was a friendly, it was a fucking friendly.'

I reflect on how Taylor made David Platt captain, and Paul is a better bloody midfielder than Platt will ever be. I look at him and think: 'You are the best midfielder in the country. Of course you should captain England.'

Paul is studying the horses as they walk around the parade ring, making comments about how they look, what they have done and what they will do. I'm aware of a chugging sound coming from beyond the French windows. Harry is Paul's gardener, a man with every growing season etched into the lines of his face. He has got a big, petrol-driven lawnmower and is creating beautiful straight green lines. You could play tennis on that. It just needs a trestle table with a jug of Robinsons Barley Water to make the look complete.

As the horses are put under starter's orders, the growling becomes louder, and Paul keeps glancing over his shoulder. As the race nears its climax, Harry is right by the French windows, trimming the edges, the noise drowning the commentary. Paul leaps up, flings open the windows and shouts: 'Harry! If you don't turn that thing off now, I am going to make you eat it.' Then he runs into the middle of the garden, looks up at the sky and yells: 'I never wanted a bloody lawn in the first place!'

When the season ended, United had played sixty-two games in all competitions and lost six. We won the title with ninety-two points. We thrashed Chelsea 4–0 to win the FA Cup, winning the first Double in the club's history. When he came to sum up the season, the *Sun*'s chief sportswriter, John Sadler, underlined our defeat by 'Champions League no-hopers' Galatasaray'. There had been more than fifty victories to choose from. Nevertheless, there was fallout from that match. There had been another row between Nobby Stiles and Les Kershaw, which ended with United sacking Nobby, who had been right about Galatasaray. They kept Les. Nobby said United would never win the European Cup playing the way they were. The fact that he had actually been part of the team that won the competition didn't seem to count for much. In fact, when he mentioned it, it was held against him.

The club also got rid of Jim McGregor. He had gone to see Ferguson about renewing his contract, thinking it would be straightforward.

'I think it's time for a new face as physio, Jim. You've been here a long time. The club needs to move on.'

'Why?'

'You've had too many arguments with the club doctor, with the surgeons. I need everyone on the same side.'

'So you're sacking me?'

'I'm not sacking you, Jim. I'm just not renewing your contract.'

Jim was a physio who would stand up for himself. There are plenty of others who don't. Jim was always reluctant to clear injured players for matches and he never gave players injections before a game. If you want an injured footballer to start a match, you inject whatever part of his body is hurting with a mixture of a steroid called cortisone and a local anaesthetic. I've seen managers order their physios to give a player an injection. Ferguson was never among them, and even if he had been, Jim would have refused. I respected them for that. An injection means you don't feel the pain, but as the manager watches his player slogging his guts out, he knows that with every stride he is damaging himself. The muscle is still being torn, still being worn. The fear of losing his place drives a player to keep on taking them. Then, slowly, game by game, he collapses like a carthorse into the mud.

The Final Furlong

'I'll have the eggs Benedict, love.'

'Good choice, sir.'

'I love eggs Benedict. It's like oral sex – you never get it at home.'

Lots of raucous laughter while Steve Bruce swings round to see who it is that has embarrassed the waitress. We are having a champagne breakfast at the Four Seasons before going off to Chester races for a team day out – or 'team bonding', as the London clubs now like to call it.

Roy Keane is sitting next to me, and I'm hoping he has more breakfast than champagne. There are two Roy Keanes: Dr Jekyll Roy is good company; Mr Hyde, to name him after Manchester's biggest brewery, is not. I don't like being with him when he's drinking. When Roy has had a drink, he changes from a quiet, unassuming man with a dry wit into a bit of a lunatic. He doesn't handle booze well.

Manchester United might be the dominant force in the Premier League, but there are very few of us who are going to the World Cup in America. England haven't qualified and nor have France, which rules out Eric. Russia have qualified, but for reasons I don't pretend to understand, Andrei will not be joining them. He doesn't like the manager, apparently.

That just leaves the Irish lads, Denis Irwin and Roy. 'You'd better get used to hotels once you get to the States,' I tell Roy, sweeping my arm around the Four Seasons' dining room.

'Jeez, we'll not be staying in anything like this. Have you met the FAI? If they have their way, we'll be in a Holiday Inn right by a twelve-lane freeway. Anyway, I don't like big hotels. This is grand, of course it is, but I've been thinking about selling my place in Bowdon, you know. There's just me, and I'm rattling around it like a domino in a shoe box.'

His home, a beautiful, five-bedroomed thing, must be worth half a million, but Roy is twenty-two and living alone. It's the sort of house a high-powered executive with three children might buy. His wife's moving to Manchester after the World Cup and she's expecting their first child, so things might settle down.

There's a naivety about Roy, which probably comes from growing up in rural Ireland. When he came to Manchester United from Nottingham Forest, he didn't have a watch, so he went into a shop called Watches of Switzerland with Lee Sharpe. Its very name might have given him some idea of the prices inside, but Lee knew the guy behind the counter, so they walked in. Roy had his credit cards with him, the platinum and gold Mastercards. When he saw a watch he liked, he asked how much it was. The man behind the counter said: 'Eleven.' Roy handed over his credit card, signed the counterfoil and walked out with the watch, a solid gold Rolex. He thought it had cost £1,100, but he'd misread the price tag. It was £11,000. He was sufficiently embarrassed that he asked Lee to promise not to tell anyone about what had just happened. He obviously didn't know Lee very well, because the first thing he did when he arrived at training was to announce it to everybody.

Roy is an exceptional player in an exceptional team. He will dominate Old Trafford, and not just Old Trafford. He will be going to America for the World Cup with Ireland, but I think the tournament in which he will shine will be the 1996 European Championships. They will be held in England on pitches Roy is familiar with and in stadiums he knows. He will be nearly twenty-five. He could be the star of that tournament and show everyone he is world class, that he is the best player in Europe. That will be the measure of the man. I'm assuming the Irish will qualify.*

---

* Ireland did not qualify for Euro 96. After the 1994 World Cup, Roy Keane never played in another international tournament.

After the racing, we went back to a hotel called the International, which has a balcony from where you can look down at the bar and lobby. There were some Scousers on it and pretty soon they were throwing beer down on us. Eric Cantona and Paul Ince were standing together, and Incey's jacket was covered in the stuff.

Paul didn't notice, but Eric did. Eric is one of those footballers who, even more than Roy, I would not like to provoke. A look comes across his face, and you know that not only is he going to lash out, there is nothing you can do to stop him. He began walking towards the men. To make matters worse, Roy appeared from nowhere. They walked towards the staircase like two cowboys marching through a saloon, looking straight ahead. The Scousers started to edge back. Everything exploded. Roy, Paul and Eric ran up the stairs, followed by four of the hotel's security staff. The bouncers dragged the three players off the Scousers and pulled them downstairs. Roy rounded on them and had to be dragged outside by the rest of the team.

And now we were looking at each other. Sweaty, suits dishevelled, a crowd starting to gather. Steve Bruce arrived, took charge and went to see the hotel manager, who said he would keep it quiet. It wouldn't be in the International's interest to make this public.

Naturally, it made the papers the next day, with Incey accused of attacking this guy, ripping his shirt and twisting his arm. There are threats to sue United, although on what grounds, I am none too sure.

There is no piece of gossip about Manchester United that is too trivial for the press to print. The club sells tabloid newspapers as effectively as *Coronation Street*. The difference is that Granada Television has a press office and a media department. We have to handle everything ourselves, and since the manager has now banned contact with the press, we have become a closed shop. The papers have responded by making stuff up. The *Sun* is not going to print a blank page with the headline: 'Sorry, Folks, We Weren't Able to Get Any United News Today'.

It's a war we cannot win.

Nice Guys

Bryan Robson won't have to organise another barbecue. He is leaving to become manager of Middlesbrough.

They are suddenly a club with a lot of money, not far from where he grew up in County Durham, and he will bring something Middlesbrough have not had since Brian Clough played for them: glamour. A perfect finish, don't you think?

Not quite. Football doesn't really do Hollywood endings, and Robbo didn't get his. We had made the FA Cup final. Just as we had in 1990, we played Oldham in the semi-finals. Just as we had four years ago, we played badly. We were one minute away from being knocked out when Mark Hughes equalised with a volley.

Although the two clubs are less than ten miles apart, the semi-final had been played at Wembley. The replay was rather more sensibly scheduled for Maine Road. This time we were utterly ruthless. We won 4–1. Bryan was among the scorers. We will play Chelsea at Wembley.

On the day before the final, the manager called Robbo into his hotel room and told him he could go out and have a drink because he wouldn't be involved at all. It was a choice between him or Lee Sharpe on the bench, and Sharpe had a future at Manchester United, although as it turned out, not that much of one. Ferguson even tried to give him money to pay for some drinks. Robbo pushed the notes away. He didn't need or want them. It was like that scene in *Goodfellas* when, towards the end, Paulie, the Mafia boss, pushes a wad of dollars into the hands of Ray Liotta's character, Henry Hill. It's his way of telling Henry, who has worked for Paulie for years, who has killed for him, that he has no more use for him. Henry looks at the notes and thinks: 'He's given me thirty-two hundred bucks for a lifetime.'

We demolished Chelsea. We were three up with twenty minutes to play. Bryan could have come on for the last fifteen minutes, taken his bow, lifted the FA Cup for the fourth time and then, after thirteen years at Manchester United, headed back to the north-east. We don't often get the finish we deserve, but that should have been his.

If Bryan makes a success of Middlesbrough, we all think he will come back to Old Trafford as manager. He knows the club, knows the ropes, and the United fans will follow him everywhere.*

I once had a brief conversation with Ferguson about who he thought might succeed him. He believed that whoever took over would need two years to bed in. He expected to be around to help Robbo or whoever it was settle in at Old Trafford. I don't think he wanted a clean break. Maybe he'll be like Matt Busby – he'll never quite leave. One day, ten years from now, a reserve goalkeeper will be walking along a deserted corridor, decide to open a door and find Ferguson staring back at him from behind a dusty desk. The guardian of Old Trafford.

Like Robbo, I've also been told I am surplus to requirements. I'll miss these people. I won't remotely encounter anything like Manchester United again.

I had been to see the manager in February. There was a chance I could play in Japan, where substantial money was being offered to European players. I may have been a reserve keeper, but I was Manchester United's reserve keeper, and that made me a bit of a catch. Gerry Payton, who had kept goal for Fulham and Bournemouth and been number two to Luděk Mikloško at West Ham, had got himself a very well-paid gig as a goalkeeping coach in Kobe.

I wondered what I might encounter in Japan. One of my

---

* In this the United players were entirely wrong. By the time Ferguson retired in 2013, Robson had been out of English football for five years.

favourite films is called *Mr Baseball*. It stars Tom Selleck as a baseball player, probably the same age as me, who is given the chance of a last big-money move to Japan. I must have watched it two or three times. I imagine I won't be asked if I've ever slept with Madonna, as Selleck was in that film. I might just be very, very lonely in a hotel room twenty floors up.

I saw the manager in his office. 'I don't mind if you let me go. I know I'm thirty-six, but I need you to know that I want to carry on playing. If you let me know now, I can put myself about with other clubs. It'll give me a head start.'

He looked straight at me. 'I'm not looking to release you. I'd like Gary Walsh to get another club.'

I mentioned the conversation to Brian Kidd. 'Well, that's you sorted then, Cat.' Based on that, we sold our house in Chingford because the kids were settled in Wilmslow. I told the people who had contacted me about Japan that I'd be staying in Manchester another season. In all the years I'd known Alex Ferguson, I could always trust him.

United's problem with Gary was that after every reserve game his knee would swell up. If he did find another club, passing a medical and getting him some insurance might be something of a problem. They didn't sell Gary, and that became a problem for me.

At the end of April, we win the Manchester derby and then beat Leeds 2–0 at Elland Road. We are two points clear of Blackburn, but they have only two matches left and we have a game in hand. On the Friday, Ferguson calls me into his office at the Cliff.

'I'll not be putting you on the bench for the final – I don't think you're competition for Peter.'

'Well, gaffer, I was on the bench for the semi-final and I don't think I was much competition for him then. I wasn't much competition for him in October. Why are you telling me this now?'

He didn't say it, but I knew he blamed me for the defeat in the League Cup final.

I played my last two games for the reserves. No sooner had I been demoted than Peter was injured at Ipswich. Gary was in goal at Old Trafford on the Wednesday night, when we beat Southampton 2–0 to retain the title. My contract was not renewed.

Like Jim Leighton before me and so many others after, Manchester United has passed me by. It was everything, and now it is a blur in the rear-view mirror.

People say to me: 'You know Alex Ferguson then?'

I always reply: 'I've been managed by him but I don't know him.'

I don't think many people do. I've been reasonably close to him for four years. I've sat on the bench with him for God knows how many games, but I can't tell you what lies beneath the skin of the man. He used to talk to me a bit more than he would to the other players partly because

I was older and partly because, well, I was the reserve goalkeeper. I was around him a bit more.

On one occasion we were having coffee in a hotel before an away game, and he told me that once he had made up his mind to get rid of a player, he never changed it. He never paced the corridors turning the decision over in his mind. 'You can't go home and worry about the player, what's happening to them or their wives and families. You've made the decision,' he said. 'You've made it for two reasons. Firstly, you've made it for yourself, because players who aren't good enough or aren't motivated enough will get you the sack. But, mainly, you've made it for the sake of the club. It's a business, football, and if you're ever a manager, Les, you remember that.'

That is why nice guys do not make good managers. It's why they tend to last six months. Once a nice guy has decided to get rid of someone, he does pace the corridors, he does turn it over in his mind, he does think of the player's family. He wonders if they have a big mortgage, if the player will get another club. So he gives the player another few games to prove himself. But he keeps on playing badly, the games are lost and the nice guy gets the sack.

Alex Ferguson is an extraordinary man. To his fingertips, he is a football man. But he is not a nice man. Ron Atkinson's not a nice man either, in case you're wondering. He's wonderful company, a great laugh, but if he needs to, he'll cut you dead.

Low Tide

I am in Blackpool, a town synonymous with cheap, vulgar attractions. There's one cheap, vulgar attraction that I've got to know particularly well: Blackpool Football Club. Do I like to be beside the seaside? Not really.

I was given a free transfer by Manchester United in the summer of 1994 and went from a club who had won the Double to one that had escaped relegation to the bottom division by a point.

When I was told I was surplus to requirements at Old Trafford, I was thirty-six, coming up to thirty-seven. There was no way I was going to find another Premier League club. I might have got a First Division club – as they call themselves these days – but the most I could have expected was a one-year contract. When I met the Blackpool chairman, Owen Oyston, he offered a bit more. Or he seemed to. Oyston owns radio stations and magazines and helps runs the Miss World shows. He kept talking about what he was going to do for Blackpool. I was impressed by him.

You bloody idiot, Les. I could have gone to Burnley or Stockport. Or some other team with half a defence. A friend rang and offered me the chance to play in Hong Kong. It was too late, I had already signed. Dave Jones, who was Stockport's assistant manager, phoned. 'I'm sorry we weren't quick enough,' he said. 'But let me tell you, that team is absolutely useless. You're going to get belted every week.'

At Blackpool, it is always 1953. It is still the Matthews Final, and on the terraces at Bloomfield Road they refuse to step into the 1990s. I must have heard the name Stanley Matthews mentioned seven hundred times in my first couple of weeks here. I have news for the good people of Blackpool: Stanley Matthews is never going to play for the club again, and neither is Stan Mortensen. The whole place reeks of the past.

When Blackpool did develop a top-class player in Trevor Sinclair, they sold him to Queens Park Rangers. The fans pay their money to slaughter the club. They have no other interest or purpose. If I were Oyston, I would not put a single penny into this football club. In his first year as chairman, he invested £800,000. Over the next three, he has put in another £700,000. All he has got for his money is aggravation.

I was signed by Sam Allardyce on a two-year contract. Sam had been a centre-half for Bolton and Sunderland, but this was his first shot at management in England. He put me straight into the team for his first match, at home to Huddersfield. We lost 4–1. The Blackpool fans began calling for the previous manager, Billy Ayre, to be reinstated – a man who had won twenty-six games out of ninety-two and nearly got the club relegated to the fourth tier.

The next game was at Bournemouth. We travelled down on the Friday evening, spending five and a half hours on the coach, stayed the night at the Bournemouth Post House and took the coach straight back after the game. We got back at half past eleven on Saturday night.

When I was warming up for the game at Dean Court, I made a couple of saves, and behind me I could hear one of the Blackpool supporters shouting: 'You'd better save that for the fucking game.' Then someone else, a balding bloke with a middle-aged spread jutting through his T-shirt, shouted: 'Sealey, you are nothing but a has-been.'

I turned round and yelled: 'I am a has-been. Don't you think I don't know that? Do you think I'd be here otherwise? But who are you? Compared with what I am, you're the Invisible Man. You've done nothing with your life. You've just travelled five hours to have an argument with someone you've never bloody met.'

We won the match 2–1.

The fans don't fancy me; they don't fancy my accent. To them I am a big-city wide boy who won't shut up about how crap this club is.

The next away game was at Chesterfield in the League Cup. My last away game in the League Cup was the final, playing for Manchester United. I let in three against Aston Villa at Wembley and let in four in the rather more humble surroundings of Saltergate. The results were linked. Blackpool fans thought they were getting United's number-two goalkeeper. They were, but they were also getting a goalkeeper who had played one and a half matches in eighteen months. I didn't even play much reserve team football, I just sat on the bench. Because of that I made mistakes. At Wembley, it took me too long to pick up the speed of the ball. Now, I'm still coming to terms with the curve and dip of crosses – and they are different in this league. I missed one against Chesterfield and they scored, and as I sat on my haunches, I asked myself: 'Les, what the hell are you doing here?'

Another goal we conceded came from a back-pass which absolutely sold me short. In the *Blackpool Gazette*, I was blamed for 'hesitation'. I wish I had hesitated more when signing that contract.

The Third Division – to give Endsleigh League Division Two its proper name – is a hard league for a bad team. It is very hard, very physical and played at speed. The message is to get the ball up the park as quickly as possible. The emphasis is not on footballing ability but on physical fitness. I understand very easily how a footballer could drop from the Premier League to this level and fail.

Blackpool's training ground is at Squires Gate, right by the sea. It's ramshackle. I have no idea where Oyston's money has gone because when I turned up for pre-season, there was no training kit. We had to bring our own. When we arrive in the mornings, there is no tea, which might sound ridiculously trivial, but when the players get together before training over a cup of tea, they can have a laugh and a joke. It adds to the team spirit.

I live quite near the training ground and drive there in my full kit, train and then go home to have a shower. That's it. I am better paid than most of the players, who are on a few hundred pounds a week. The win bonus is a lavish £45. At United, the players would go out when they got their win bonuses and they might buy themselves a new jacket. Here, it would stretch to a pair of socks.

Allardyce works as hard as any manager I have ever come across, but he is up against Blackpool's history, and I don't think he realised this before he signed his contract. I'm not sure he would have come to Bloomfield Road had he known. He is trying to get us to play the correct way with a sweeper system. He has the right ideas, but does he have time?

If I were him, I'd put most of this team up for sale. I'd get rid of them. But you can't at this level, because if you don't manage to sell them, your career as a manager is in the hands of people you have just told you don't want. You'd lie awake at night thinking about that.

I've just been told that Dave Bamber, who is Blackpool's centre-forward – and a good one at that – is going to be put in as a makeshift centre-half on Saturday. I wouldn't mind being dropped for that one.

I rang the *Blackpool Gazette* to tell them what I thought of the state of the club. I told the reporter, who I think knows nothing about football, what a mess the club was in. I said I didn't care if the supporters booed me, just so long as they came and watched.

When I picked up the paper, my criticisms of the club and the fans had been totally watered down. The article had no bite. It said I was asking for time, which I wasn't. I know how time works in football: it is always later than you think.

When I was released by United, Andrei Kanchelskis had come over to me and said: 'Don't worry, you'll be all right, *koshka*.' I wish I were.

Koshka is Russian for 'cat', and that is what Andrei called me. I loved him. I first met him in 1991, just before the Cup Winners' Cup final. He'd come on trial from Shakhtar Donetsk and turned up in an old tracksuit which looked like a pair of overalls. He had his boots in his hand. They were not even his own. He had actually come to Manchester United on trial from Ukraine and not brought any football boots. He was told to go to a sports shop and buy a pair.

He couldn't speak a word of English and looked lost in this big, glittery town. What he could do was keep banging balls into the corner of a net. He had one of the hardest shots I have ever faced. The balls swerved, dipped and fizzed past you. Once he advanced on goal, he no longer looked a lost boy; he looked like a man completely at home, completely confident in his own abilities.

When I returned to United in 1993, Andrei told me the first words he had picked up were 'shite' and 'fuck off'. If he scored when we were practising shooting at the Cliff, he would say: '*Koshka*, shite,' or '*Koshka*, fuck off.' As he left the changing rooms, you could see his wardrobe had been transformed. Now he was clad in Versace, head to toe. Everything.

He had bought this left-hand drive Mercedes so he could take it back to Ukraine, although that would have had to have been an epic drive. I don't think he's ever going back to Donetsk. When he first arrived with it at the Cliff, he called me over. '*Koshka*, come see car. Look, leather seats.' He stroked them as if they had been made with the last piece of leather on Earth. 'Air conditioning, three-speed. Sunroof, electric windows. *Koshka*, Andrei's car is magnificent.'

During the summer, a mate of mine was asked to fit some carpets in Andrei's house. When Andrei came home, he told my mate and his helper to stop work. They did, thinking they must have the wrong colour or wrong material. Instead, Andrei told them to sit at the dining-room table, and his wife brought them a banquet – course upon course of food. Ireland were on television playing in the

World Cup, and Andrei said: 'We sit, we smoke cigars and we watch football.' They did. The two men didn't finish laying the carpet until 11pm. Andrei had quite a lonely life here, and he just wanted some company, someone to watch some football with.

Apart from Roy Keane and Denis Irwin, Manchester United had nobody at the World Cup. France didn't qualify, which was a pity because now that FIFA have outlawed the tackle from behind, the World Cup would have suited Eric Cantona.

He is the one person in the United dressing room who has never felt the wrath of Alex Ferguson's tongue. Even when he's played badly, the manager never says anything to him, hardly ever gives him instructions. Usually, he's just told to get on with his game. Ferguson seems to be genuinely wary of him, as if he knows Eric has turned his back on so many people in his career. He doesn't want to be the next, so he is indulged. When Ferguson's eldest son, Mark, presented him with his first grandchild, the manager was visibly thrilled. He almost skipped into training, and when he opened the dressing-room door, Brian McClair turned to him and said: 'How's little Eric doing then?'

Eric is full of contradictions. The image he projects on the pitch, with his collar turned up, is of a man alone. Heathcliff on the moors. He is nothing of the sort. If the team goes out, whether it's to a race meeting, a restaurant or a nightclub, you'll usually find Eric with us. He is up for a good time, and given the pressure he's under, I'm not surprised. He must crave a release.

I have never been in a car with Eric, and given the state of his motor, I have no wish to. It's small, unpretentious, dirty and scuffed. It looks like he has reversed into something more than once. Yet he told me that back home in France, he has a blue Rolls-Royce Corniche convertible and a Harley-Davidson. Both, he says, are immaculate and kept in a garage.

A couple of days after we beat Chelsea in the FA Cup final, Mark Hughes was awarded a testimonial, against Celtic. We all turned up in club blazers and ties. Eric arrived in a baseball cap and ripped jeans. Then he will turn up at a function where there's no specific dress code in a beautiful Balmain suit and an immaculately tailored overcoat, looking like a film star. He is genuinely interested in acting and the theatre. One thing he never discusses with us in the dressing room is football, and I have the impression that if Eric were not a footballer, he wouldn't watch it or be particularly enthralled by it.

Yet he is the best player I have ever seen, certainly in that position. He's the reason Manchester United are now the most successful club in England. Eric has hardened United, made them tougher, and he's also brought something more subtle: the players see Eric trying new things in training, so they try them too – and not just at the Cliff. He's made the team more inventive, and United no longer have that very English fear of trying something new or unusual.

He once told me he would never go back to play in France because he doesn't think the game there is straight. It can be bought and sold, and the match-fixing charges against Marseilles after the 1993 European Cup final suggest he might be right. They were playing Milan in the final and didn't want to pick up any injuries beforehand, so in the last league game of the season they bribed their opponents not to make too many tackles.

Marseilles is where Eric's from. He was in Manchester when all that happened, but by then he loathed the club. He played for them for three years, the boyhood dream and all that. They dropped him for the 1991 European Cup final and the Coupe de France final. Not to the bench but from the squad. Marseilles lost both matches, by the way. He will not be going back because Eric never goes where he is not appreciated, and that's one thing Manchester gives him, something that I don't think he's had anywhere else: people who understand him.

He does what he wants. If he ever felt unhappy at Manchester United, or felt like he had done enough, he would just walk out. If he walks away from United, he will walk away from football altogether. When he does, he will be impossible to replace.

Now I'm at Blackpool I miss the backroom staff, people like Jimmy Curran, who is the assistant physio and fancies himself as a singer in the Frank Sinatra/Sammy Davis Jr mould. He performs in working men's clubs and nightclubs and is forever terrified the team will turn up to have a go at him. He was always very careful not to let us know where he was appearing. I've got a cassette of some of his songs, and he's not bad.

I even miss Teresa, a smashing Irish lady who does the cooking at the Cliff. Apart from the lovely thick custard that went very well with a jam roly-poly, the food United would serve their players was absolutely terrible. You could pebble-dash a house with Teresa's semolina, and I used to tell her that if she really could produce 'home-made lasagne' in thirteen minutes, then she was some kind of miracle worker. We would take our plates back and say: 'Thanks, Teresa, that was fucking horrible.' She would always laugh and say: 'Oh, get away with you.' I have got away, Teresa. To a place that's a damn sight worse than your cooking.

I do sometimes wonder what will happen to Daisy and Dolly. I don't think Gary Pallister will do anything once he retires. He's paid a lot and doesn't squander his cash. Certainly not on clothes. There will be no need for him to work once he leaves Old Trafford. To show you how careful Gary is with money, he once decided to buy himself a Toyota Supra Turbo. Top of the range. £37,000. He knew I was in the car game. His first question to me was not who designed the bodywork or the engine, it was how much a Toyota Supra Turbo would depreciate by in twelve months. I had him on, pretended that in three years' time it would be worth only £12,000. Gary had apoplexy and nearly decided not to buy it. I see him driving it sometimes, wearing Ray-Ban sunglasses, as if he imagines himself as Schwarzenegger barrelling down Rodeo Drive, an image slightly spoiled by his insistence on sucking lollipops as he drives.

I can imagine Steve Bruce working in the media, sitting alongside Des Lynam in the studio. He is very good with the press. He's very intelligent, always got time for questions after a game and is a very good communicator. The one thing about Steve that I could never understand was England's refusal to pick him. Whenever there was an international break, it would sometimes be just me, Mike Phelan and Steve in the dressing room at the Cliff. Mike and I would both be wondering what Steve was doing there.

I never got close to becoming an international footballer. My biggest fault was that I was never a good goalkeeper, technically. I'm using the past tense because once I left United in 1994, there was only one direction in which my career would be heading. I never possessed that spark of genius that Pat Jennings or Peter Shilton had. I saved the ball with anything I could, whether it was my hands, my head or my arse. It didn't matter, as long as the ball stayed out of the net.

I had two great attributes. Firstly, I had a pure enthusiasm for the game. I would play anywhere. Whenever I took my two sons out, it would nearly always end up with a game of football. The other was that I was never afraid of being hurt. I always went in where the boots were flying. I had my great slice of luck in 1990, being on loan at Old Trafford when Alex Ferguson had to make a choice and everything was on a knife-edge for him and for Manchester United. Otherwise, I would have been a very small postscript in the history of Luton Town, remembered by some of the old-timers as a competent goalkeeper in a relatively successful team.

The gulf between success and failure is bigger at United than anywhere I have ever played. If you are successful, or even if you're liked, you become a god. If you fail, they will destroy you. Just as I knew, deep down, that I would never play for England, I recognised I was not quite good enough for Manchester United. I was there to fill a gap until the next great goalkeeper came to Old Trafford. But they did like me, and I knew that if I stayed in that team, my bank manager would like me too. I was determined to fill that space not with money but with all those experiences that I would never have had unless I'd come to United.

I love goalkeepers. I have never met one without a personality. They may be funny, they may be different, but they are nearly always odd. The good ones certainly are. As they become older, they become odder. If I could describe a goalkeeper to you, I would say he is a madman trying to be sane.

Goalkeepers are men alone. Other players are wary of them, particularly in dressing rooms before a game. They like things the rest of the players don't like, they laugh at things the others don't find amusing. The worst audience for a stand-up comic would be a room full of keepers.

One goalkeeper I know has his wife keeping files on all the strikers he is likely to face in the season. She watches all the videos, reads all the match reports and compiles a mini-library. There are details on how they hit a ball, how they shape up to take free kicks and where they place their penalties (it's not my wife, in case you're wondering).

Before latex gloves arrived, John Burridge would sew small Brillo pads into the fingers and thumbs of his cotton gloves because they would give him a better grip. On the coach to an away game, John would ask his Newcastle teammates to randomly throw an orange or tangerine at him without warning to keep his reflexes sharp. Nobody would want to room with him because, in the middle of the night, he would get up and start diving across his bed.

Neville Southall would travel separately from his Everton teammates. He would be driven to the ground, change before anyone else arrived and start practising. He became one of the best goalkeepers in the world. He collects clocks.

Some keepers, like Ray Clemence or Bruce Grobbelaar, were very laid-back in training. Ray barely touched the ball; Bruce would play up front in five-a-sides. They just trusted to their natural ability. That takes some self-belief, let me tell you.

The best goalkeeper I have ever seen was Rinat Dasayev, who played for Spartak Moscow and the Soviet Union. He made it very young: he was twenty-two when he won the Soviet championship. Because he lived in a communist system, there were few distractions. All that mattered was goalkeeping. In 1988, he got a move to Seville. Three thousand fans met him at the airport. He was nicknamed the 'Iron Wall' and was paid more money than he had ever seen in his life. There were clothes, cars, cash to burn. Women. His performances fell apart and he damaged his fingers in a car crash. I hope the West gives Andrei a better outcome.

By the way, there's something I've been meaning to tell you. I've had a call from Harry Redknapp. Harry Redknapp who played in midfield at Upton Park. Harry Redknapp who is now manager of West Ham United. In the Premier League.

He wants me as cover for Luděk Mikloško. I'm going home. Back to where all this began.

The Castle

Joe and Nicole married in Castle Hedingham, a chocolate-box village in north Essex which had once been at the centre of more violence and power than Fort Vallance.

It was the home of the de Vere family, the earls of Oxford. One had been a guarantor of the Magna Carta; another had been the lover of the doomed boy king Richard II. One had directed the archers at Agincourt; another, John, having picked the wrong side in the Wars of the Roses, had been castrated, disembowelled and then beheaded on Tower Hill. He followed his elder son Aubrey to the scaffold. His younger son, also called John, had led Henry Tudor's army at Bosworth and killed Richard III, the brother of the man who had ordered the execution of his father and brother. Compared to John de Vere, the revenge Ronnie Kray exacted in the Blind Beggar had been ordinary.

Fort Vallance had been demolished in 1988. Most of Hedingham Castle had gone the same way. Only its great keep, with its eleven-foot-thick walls, had survived, but it had lasted well enough to stage banquets and weddings, and it was here that Joe and Nicole, two survivors, were married. Elaine, too, had shown herself to be a survivor. Unlike her son, she had not escaped drugs or alcohol but something far more cruel and pernicious.

The lymphatic system is a series of highways that carry white blood cells, the lymphocytes, which protect the body from infection. Like the London Underground, the system has interchange points where the lines connect. The equivalents to Baker Street, Bank and Oxford Circus are in the groin, the armpit and the neck: the lymph nodes.

In 2000, the former Arsenal midfielder David Rocastle was in Borneo. He had played for the island's biggest team, Sabah, brought his family over, enjoyed the lifestyle and even learned a little Malay. However, his knees would not stand for any more football, not even at this level. There was an offer from his agent, Jerome Anderson, to come back to London and work for him, while the Arsenal vice-chairman, David Dein, wanted him to return to the club and coach its youth teams.

In his bathroom, Rocastle noticed two lumps in his armpit. When he returned to England, he was told he had something called non-Hodgkin lymphoma. The lymphocytes in his body were multiplying abnormally and, stripped of their power to fight infection, were collecting in his lymph nodes. His body, honed and athletically beautiful, was defenceless against infection.

Rocastle died in March 2001. He was thirty-three. This footballer's funeral came a few months before Les Sealey's, this time in Windsor. Tony Adams, Alan Smith and Michael Thomas, a few of the men with whom Rocastle had helped Arsenal snatch the title at Liverpool on the last night of the 1988/9 season, carried his coffin.

Elaine's encounter with non-Hodgkin lymphoma came in that queasy period between Christmas and New Year 2006, when everyone knows the date but no one is very sure of the day. She lifted her arms in the bathroom and discovered a lump. Shortly after Les's death, she had begun suffering from waves of almost complete exhaustion, mixed in with the shock and stress of losing her husband. Elaine was diagnosed with anaemia and prescribed iron tablets.

Four years later, the intense weariness that seemed to drag her down with every step was back. This time there were night sweats, and now there was something beneath her skin. She had to see someone.

Elaine was taken to the Princess Alexandra Hospital in Harlow. The lump was cut out and pronounced non-cancerous. However, her blood counts were all over the place. Every sample produced a different number of white cells. A haematologist was called in. A scan showed an enlarged spleen, but the consultants at the Princess Alexandra were convinced it was not caused by cancer. This certainty lasted nine months, until a sample of bone marrow revealed that Elaine had non-Hodgkin lymphoma. It is a cancer that can spread outside the lymphatic system. There are usually two routes it chooses: one is to the liver; the other is to the spleen. The spleen can be removed; the liver cannot. David Rocastle's entered his liver and killed him; Elaine's went to her spleen, which was surgically removed. Chemotherapy was administered at Harlow every three weeks, and the cancer was stamped out. Elaine was, however, told that she might never be free of it.

It stayed away for six years. She knew it was back before the doctors did. She could sense its ways: the sudden onset of exhaustion, the soaking pillows from the night sweats.

Chemotherapy is not a single treatment; it is a cocktail menu. Pancreatic cancer is treated with a mixture of gemcitabine and FOLFIRINOX; doxorubicin and cyclophosphamide are used against breast cancer. Each medication has a side effect. There are five separate drugs that make up the chemotherapy for non-Hodgkin lymphoma. One is rituximab, which encourages the body's immune system to attack cancer cells. Its side effect is hair loss. When Elaine was told she would lose her hair, she cried for a week. At a meeting to discuss the treatment, she said: 'Am I really going to lose my hair this time?'

As people around the table nodded, Elaine broke down once more. A junior doctor leaned forward. 'But, Mrs Sealey, when we confirmed the cancer had returned, you were fine. I don't understand what it is about your hair.'

Elaine's hair was long and blonde. It had been long and blonde since she was a child. It was a part of her, and it would come out in great clumps, although when it did, she was strangely calm about it. It was the thought of it falling out that had been upsetting.

Elaine had a full head of hair for the wedding on 17 May 2008. It was Cup final day. Portsmouth, managed by Harry Redknapp, beat Cardiff.

As Elaine reminded her son before the ceremony, 17 May was the anniversary of another cup final: the replay between Manchester United and Crystal Palace, when Les Sealey had stepped out of the tunnel at Wembley, faced the music and danced.

The Priory

It was the Olympic summer of 2012. The first full day. The night before had seen the Opening Ceremony. Images of Glastonbury Tor, of the great chimneys of the Industrial Revolution, of nurses bouncing on NHS beds, of the Queen and James Bond parachuting into the stadium in Stratford.

A few miles away, Joe Sealey was in the garden of the family house in Chigwell. With him was a bottle of Dom Pérignon and some cocaine. Marriage had not cured him of his addiction. Nicole was not at home. He would go out into London, a city that suddenly felt young, vibrant and optimistic. It would be quite something to share in all of that.

Hours later, he was in a hotel in Holborn, staring at a hairdryer. He had checked in, as he did when he wanted to surrender himself to cocaine. There had been plenty of booze and conversations with random Australians whom he had met in the pubs, but now it was time. This is what he had come out for.

Then, in a moment of clarity, he realised that he would have to explain his whereabouts to Nicole. She could tell, just by how he looked, by how he spoke, whether Joe had been using. Sometimes Nicole would ring him at random times and know whether he was clean or not just by how he said 'hello'.

It was the early hours of the morning. A time often reserved for death, for childbirth. A time for flashes of insight and truly dreadful decisions. If Joe hit himself in the face with the hairdryer, hit himself hard, he could tell Nicole he had been in a fight and had spent the night in a police cell. If he aimed carefully – and in this state, he knew it would be hard to do so – he might give himself a black eye, which would give his story ammunition. But he was just sober enough to realise he might succeed only in blinding himself. He would sleep this off, go home and forge an arrest sheet on his computer. That would be considerably less painful.

Nicole was still out when he got back to Chigwell, but one phone call, one 'hello' was all it took for her to know. There was a heated, furious exchange. Then silence, followed by another call. Nicole had been in touch with the Priory. They had a bed. They could take him. That afternoon.

The Priory looked like something out of *Downton Abbey*,

a Georgian manor house in its own parkland. Ionic columns greeted you at the entrance. Joe was taken to his bedroom via a series of doors, their entrances protected by codes.

A doctor came in to assess whether he was a suitable case for treatment. Since he would be paying £25,000 for a month inside this building, Joe found it hard to imagine why they wouldn't accept him. The assessment involved three questions and took five minutes. They would accept him. The cocaine and vodka were still clawing at his brain. Joe realised he hadn't eaten for three days. They brought him a bowl of fruit. He was told this was unusual – the Priory didn't allow you to snack. There would be three meals a day, all eaten communally. All coffee was decaffeinated.

Despite the opulence of the exterior, there was no gym, no swimming pool, and his phone had already been surrendered. It took time to orientate himself, but Joe discovered there were two groups of patients. One had been referred to the Priory under the Mental Health Act: schizophrenics, self-harmers, people on suicide watch. They had table tennis and pool tables. His group, the addicts, had hours of therapy.

He began to assess the people he was with. One young woman was, to quote a song by Robert Palmer, addicted to love. Every time she met a man, every time he smiled at her or bought her dinner or gifts, he became a saviour. Once he did anything outside the confines of a romantic novel, he became the devil.

There was a seventeen-year-old princess from the

Arabian Gulf, who had been caught with drugs in her car. Joe wondered what she was doing there. She did not seem especially addicted; the drugs had been a bit of fun. Her mother, however, thought three months in the Priory was the minimum requirement. There was an ex-QC in his seventies who had all but drowned himself in brandy. A marketing executive who ran marathons barefoot until his feet bled. There were gamblers, alcoholics, sex addicts, drug users. One man from Guernsey had a full house – he was into the lot.

There were no celebrities. They tended to use the original Priory, in Roehampton, south-west London. This one was in Southgate, in the north of the city. The treatment was the same: a twelve-step programme that began with an admission that you were an addict and the addiction was beyond your control. You were not allowed to touch anyone. If someone started crying, you were not supposed to pass them a tissue. The patients were not to be over-helped.

Joe found the routine of the Priory simple to cope with. You were told where to go, when to eat, what time you had a meeting. It was like being back at Chadwell Heath with West Ham. The therapists were non-judgemental. They did not give a view or express an opinion on what Joe told them. They were there to guide him, but the journey had to be his.

Dorrit was an exception. She was not little but big, motherly and Jewish. If you said something idiotic, she would tell you. Usually, when Joe mentioned his father had played for Manchester United or that he had once been on West Ham's books, the conversation would soften. People would be interested; it would give him an edge in the conversation. Dorrit could not care less.

The patients were allowed out once a week. Every Friday, they would be driven to some stables about ten miles away. There, they would have horse therapy. They would stroke the horses, put a bridle, saddle or head collar on them. Joe sat next to Dorrit, who was driving the Ford Galaxy people carrier, and told her that he would be checking out as soon as they returned to Southgate. He had done enough therapy. He could cope.

She turned to him. 'Do you love your wife?'

'Yeah, of course.'

'If you leave, you will die.'

He stayed.

At five o'clock on the twenty-eighth day, Joe was allowed to leave. Before he went out with Nicole into the gardens, before he stepped back into the noise that made up the real world, there was a final meeting for them both to attend. Joe was asked what he expected to discover when he returned home. This was a question he could answer precisely. What he expected to discover was on top of a cupboard in the kitchen. It was a small bag of cocaine.

When they got home, he stood on tiptoes and felt for it. It was there, soft and comforting. He consumed it within a day of coming home.

Inside a week, he was back facing the columns and the brown stone facade of the Priory. Suddenly, there was a roar of an engine, a squeal of wheels, and Joe turned around just in time to see a car trying to run him down. He leaped out of the way with a couple of seconds to spare. The car was being driven by his wife. Nicole had dropped him off just a few minutes before.

There were many reasons he stopped this slow suicide. He was exhausted by a decade and more of grief, this endless wake for his father. Mostly, it was because he was tired of saying sorry. He was sick of hurting his wife, apologising from the pit of his stomach and then hurting her again. There were two ways in which he could stop all this. One was to die. The other was to live. He decided to live.

His Father's Voice

Sunday, 24 August 2014

The road leading to the training ground of the biggest football club in the world was a long stretch of single-track concrete. If a Porsche Cayenne met a Range Rover there would be no way through. It reinforced the feeling that Manchester United was a club that liked to keep people out. Carrington was an unattractive part of Greater Manchester. In a playing field were shaggy, unkempt horses that made you wonder if they belonged to someone or had been abandoned there. It was a place of electricity pylons, power stations and small factories.

Les had trained at the Cliff in Salford, where people could and did turn up to watch. Remi, his grandson, would be turning out for United's under-13s in sleeker, more secret surroundings. As he watched, Joe wondered if United was right for the boy. Remi was a forward, he scored goals, but he wasn't always played as one. Sometimes he was on the wing; a few times he was placed deeper into midfield; occasionally, he would find himself employed as a full-back. Sometimes he didn't play at all. The competition here was fiercer than anywhere else in England. There was a lad called Mason Greenwood, from Bradford, who had been with United since he was six.

Everybody knew what the next step might be. These were crucial seasons, years when you had to hang in there and survive. Under-13s football guaranteed you nothing, though you could at least say you once played for Manchester United.

Three years down the line, the stakes would be higher; no longer was it a mere boast at the bar or something to mention on a date when the conversation flagged. At fifteen, you might not be offered a professional contract by the biggest club in the world, but you would be offered a contract by someone.

Joe and Nicole lived in Stapleford Abbotts, where the Shadowlands became open Essex countryside. The village had an aerodrome from which Hurricanes were flown during the war, until a V2 rocket obliterated the place. They had a good life, but as Remi grew up their evenings became full of anxious conversations about the boy. He didn't seem sharp as his mother had been sharp. He wasn't academic. There were conversations about his commitment. Remi did, however, show a passion for football.

His first proper club had been in Harold Hill, one of the hardest, most unforgiving parts of the Shadowlands. Joe had chosen it deliberately because he was told Remi had to toughen up. He needed to be kicked, jostled and pushed, mentally and physically. Harold Hill was good at toughening up people. It was one big council estate, and even at the age of ten, the boys knew football was their likeliest, perhaps their only means of escape.

Jonjo Shelvey had escaped and got himself a move to Liverpool. He'd started out in a council flat in Harold Hill. When he was a kid, his father once took him to the pub while he had a few with the lads. He bought him a Coke and some crisps, hoped there might be something on the telly to keep the boy busy. But Jonjo couldn't watch television because the TV had a bullet hole through it. He tugged at his dad's sleeve and asked if they could go.

Jonjo was now on fifteen thousand a week. At the age of twenty. His dad ran Harold Hill's football club. Scouts from the big London teams were usually pacing the touchline. When Joe first joined the scouts and began watching Harold Hill Boys, he was nervous.

At first Remi was the worst player there, but he soon became quicker, faster, more confident. He was resilient, he didn't whinge, and before long the scouts began coming over to Joe and asking if he'd like to take Remi to sessions at Tottenham or Fulham.

They ended up at Fulham, a small, friendly club. Everyone at the training ground at Motspur Park seemed to know each other. When you arrived, they asked how you were. Motspur Park was on the other side of London, near Twickenham, Teddington Lock and Hampton Court Palace. It took two hours from Stapleford Abbotts. It was two hours back, through central London. Remi would eat, do his homework and sleep in the car. Joe thought that if he kept his eyes open, he might make it as a tour guide, if the football didn't work out.

Things were changing. The late-night conversations between Joe and Nicole no longer revolved around whether Remi would make anything of his life or what he might do if the football fell through but where they should live.

Although it had been hammered by the financial crash of 2008, Nicole's company had survived and had hauled itself back up to where it had been before everything started to slide. There were vacancies at the stations for people to work in the buffets and ticket offices, but mostly the jobs involved laying and repairing track.

The biggest prize, however, lay further north. The West Coast mainline had been upgraded to run the new Pendolino trains, which tilted and turned as they took corners at 120mph. The Pendolinos and their track required plenty of maintenance. Their depot was at Longsight in Manchester's southern suburbs. An hour to the south were the great mar-shalling yards at Crewe, the fulcrum of the whole network. Nicole and Joe could set up an office in between, somewhere like Macclesfield.

'I don't know anyone up north, so it doesn't matter to me where we live,' Nicole told Joe. 'It's not as if we're tied to anywhere. But what I'm not doing is having Remi ferried around for two hours in a car to training every evening. Why don't you find him a club up there, take him up during the summer and see how he gets on? If Blackburn take him on, we'll live near Blackburn.'

Joe didn't know anyone at Blackburn, but he did vaguely know the man who ran the Manchester United academy. Brian McClair had been Alex Ferguson's second signing as manager of United. One of the early heroes, he had played alongside Les in the 1990 FA Cup final and the Cup Winners' Cup final against Barcelona.

No club treasured its young players more than United, and McClair had been overseeing their production for half a dozen years. Paul Pogba, Marcus Rashford and Jesse Lingard had all passed through his hands. Joe had met him only once, at Les's funeral, but now he found his number, pushed the buttons and talked Remi up. McClair said he should bring him along.

Man and boy headed north. They stayed at the Holiday Inn, which was by the dual carriageway that tunnels beneath the runway of Manchester Airport. Joe delighted in telling

Remi that Cristiano Ronaldo had written off his Ferrari in that tunnel. They found a place for rent in Wilmslow. It was next door to the house where Joe had lived while Les was with Manchester United. His dad would have approved of the Aston Martin dealership on the corner. Aston Martin chose the locations of their showrooms carefully: Jersey and the Isle of Man for those who found paying income tax an inconvenience; Mayfair and Chichester for those with old money; Brentwood for the Essex boys with more recent cash. Wilmslow was the capital of the Cheshire footballers' belt. There were three shops that seemed to sell nothing but sunglasses.

Joe had been coached by his father, and although he wasn't coaching Remi, he was looking out for him. He drew on his own experience: when to push the boy, when not to push. He'd tell Remi stories of how things were when he was his age.

At Carrington, Joe was watching Remi with the same mingling of pride and anxiety with which all parents watch their children, but he was also examining him critically. Did he anticipate the runs? How instinctively did he find space? There are certain things that, if you don't do them by the time you are twelve, you never will. Then, out of the corner of his eye, Joe noticed a man. Or rather, he noticed a haircut. Other than Roy Cropper from *Coronation Street*, he knew only one man with a pudding-basin haircut like that.

Les Clitheroe had run Joe's Sunday-football team. Joe had been ten then. He had not seen Les in twenty-two years, but he still recognised him.

He went over. The first thing Clitheroe said was: 'I have your dad's book.'

'Dad didn't write a book. He read a few, but as far as I know, he didn't write one.'

'Well, he sort of did, but it never came to anything. When he left United, we sat down and did some tapes. He was at Blackpool, he had time on his hands, but when he went back to London it all fell away. It's all in the loft. Been there for twenty years. If you come round, I'll fetch it for you.'

On the Tuesday, Joe drove over to Poynton, the village where he'd played football as a boy. Les handed him a blue folder containing papers scoured by pencil marks and crossings-out, and a white sandwich box, the sort that the ten-year-old Joe might have been given to take to a game. Inside, was an assortment of cassette tapes.

Joe took them home. He might as well have been given a box full of 78s. Not only did he not own a cassette player, he struggled to think of anyone who might lend him one.

On the Sunday morning, Joe drove Remi to play at Hull. As they sped along the M62, through the flatlands of east Yorkshire, there was a turn-off to Beverley. They were early; they could find a café, get a proper breakfast. Near the café was an Oxfam shop. In the window was a light blue portable tape recorder. It cost three pounds. It was no ghetto blaster, but then Beverley was a town entirely without ghettos. It looked as if it might have belonged to a girl or, judging by the fact it had a tape of *The Very Best of Matt Monro* still inside it, a woman of a certain age. It was cued up to play 'On Days Like These'.

That evening, Joe placed the cassette recorder on a desk. Suddenly, he felt afraid. Sky Sports and their need to fill schedules with repeats meant he had seen his father in action many times. Les had played in four finals for Manchester United. All had been packaged up and shown again to fill the endless afternoons. However, Les was not a man who trusted journalists. He made it a rule never to give interviews, not even for television, where the questions were banal and predictable, so Joe had not heard his father's voice since the yelled conversation on the stairs: 'Come and watch some telly with me.'

He didn't want to hear it now. He gathered up the tape recorder and the tapes and shoved them in a drawer. He would never play them.

Consequences

As a turning point in the modern history of Manchester United, the 1990 FA Cup final is eclipsed only by the Munich air disaster. Martin Edwards has confirmed that had Manchester United lost to Crystal Palace, Alex Ferguson would almost certainly have been dismissed.

Under Ron Atkinson, the club never finished lower than fourth and won the FA Cup twice. In his first three seasons at Old Trafford, Ferguson finished eleventh and thirteenth, exceeded Atkinson's total spending in a single season and won nothing. Edwards, who was involved in physical confrontations with Manchester United fans during the 1989/90 season, remarked in his autobiography, *Red Glory*, that the point was fast being reached when he could no longer keep defending Ferguson, either in the stadium or the boardroom. 'It was winning the FA Cup that saved Alex because, looking at our league form, it was still wildly indifferent. If circumstances had played out differently, Alex might very well have been pushed out of United.'

Over the next twenty-three years, the club would win two European Cups, the now-defunct Cup Winners' Cup, thirteen league titles, four more FA Cups and four League Cups. By the time he retired, Sir Alex Ferguson had become the greatest manager the British game had known.

The rift between Ferguson and Jim Leighton never healed. In 1997, after revitalising his career at Hibernian, Leighton returned to Aberdeen, where the two of them had known such glory. He was Scotland's first-choice goalkeeper for the 1998 World Cup in France, and two years later played for Aberdeen in the Scottish League Cup and Scottish Cup finals. He broke his jaw in the second of those matches, retiring from football at the age of forty-one.

Jim carried Les Sealey's coffin. The medal Les tried to give Jim in the aftermath of the cup final that changed both their lives is now on display at the Manchester United Museum.

Acknowledgements

Just as *On Days Like These* begins with a dash to hospital, so too must the Acknowledgements. On the morning of 21 October 2022, I woke up, and once my feet touched the bedroom floor, found myself entirely unable to walk. Every step I took saw me collapse. I was taken by ambulance to Salford Royal, where I was diagnosed with a mid-brain stroke. I was paralysed down the left-hand side of my body. My left leg felt like a piece of frozen meat that had no connection with the rest of my body. My left hand was like one of those metallic fairground claws that drops its prize just when it seems it's about to present you with a fluffy toy or watch. I could do nothing for myself. The sign above my bed declared: 'Hoist Only'. If I wanted to go to the toilet, I would use a commode. Otherwise, I could pee into a cardboard bottle. I had gone to bed a reasonably young-looking fifty-six. I had woken up an old man.

That the book was finished at all owes everything to the love and care I received from the staff at, first, Salford Royal, where Sir Alex Ferguson was treated for a brain haemorrhage in May 2018, and then the Stroke Rehab ward at Trafford General. To be bathed and shaved by Errol, a nurse at Salford Royal, was one of the most humbling experiences of my life. The National Health Service is nothing without its staff. I owe every one of them, at both hospitals, the greatest debt of my life. That you are holding a book that occupied me for three years is because of them. The support of my stepchildren, Rose, Jack, George, Joe and Rachel, was also critical in maintaining the optimism that I would come through and complete a book I had begun more than two years ago, when the world felt a very different place.

During the first spring of the coronavirus, a time of vivid blossom and deep blue skies, I became aware of a Tupperware box full of cassettes. The problem was that the men whose voices appear on them, Les Sealey and Les Clitheroe, were both dead. The tapes looked like something on to which I would have recorded the voices of John Peel and Janice Long, back in the evenings when David Bowie, another product of the London suburbs, rather than David Beckham was the dominant celebrity in my life.

The recordings were made in 1994, when Sealey was at a low and, it seemed, terminal phase in his career. He had been discarded by Manchester United and was playing at Blackpool in the third tier of English football. Bloomfield Road is forty miles from Old Trafford, but to Sealey it felt like another world. Collaborating with Clitheroe, who was a scout for Stellar, the football agency he had helped found, on a book must have seemed like good therapy. I am enormously grateful that he did.

The tapes, however, were not complete. There were gaps, especially around the four years Les spent at Luton. I am grateful to his constant friend, Lawrence Lustig, his former manager, David Pleat, and Elaine Sealey for filling in the gaps. I would like to thank Glen Johnson for his contribution and Harry Redknapp for providing the foreword. It was, however, a phone call from the *Daily Telegraph*'s football correspondent, Sam Wallace, that changed the course of *On Days Like These*. I confessed I was becoming dismayed by the gaps in the tapes. Sam advised me to 'become Les', in the same way that David Peace became Brian Clough in *The Damned United*. 'You have the ability to do it, so you should do it,' he said, encouragingly. The discovery of a new tape meant this became unnecessary, but it gave me the confidence to push on. *On Days Like These* is not a work of fiction, but I must confess I enjoyed trying to find Les's voice.

Another deep debt of gratitude must be with the Sealey family. Without Joe, Elaine, George and Nicole's willingness to discuss often painful details, *On Days Like These* would never have got off the ground. Joe, especially, showed enormous courage to delve into his own addictions. Thanks are due to Richard Milner and his editorial team at Quercus and my agent, David Luxton, for guiding the project to completion.

The saddest event during the writing of *On Days Like These* was the death of my wife, Sally, in January 2022, after a long and increasingly cruel struggle with pancreatic cancer. Sally, a fine journalist herself, was a constant and practical encourager of my work and had read several chapters of this book before she became too weak to continue.

During her illness, she once asked: 'Will you write about me when I'm no longer here?' In a sense, I have done, because the theme of *On Days Like These* is not just football but grief.

Tim Rich
Sale, Cheshire, February 2023

Index